DELPHI PASCAL
PROGRAMMING

EFFICIENT CODE EDITING, VISUAL DESIGNING, AND INTEGRATED DEBUGGING

4 BOOKS IN 1

BOOK 1
DELPHI PASCAL PROGRAMMING ESSENTIALS: MASTERING EFFICIENT CODE EDITING

BOOK 2
FROM BASICS TO BRILLIANCE: VISUAL DESIGNING IN DELPHI PASCAL PROGRAMMING

BOOK 3
ADVANCED TECHNIQUES IN DELPHI PASCAL: INTEGRATED DEBUGGING STRATEGIES

BOOK 4
DELPHI PASCAL PROGRAMMING PRO: FINE-TUNING CODE EDITING AND VISUAL DESIGNING FOR EXPERTS

ROB BOTWRIGHT

Published by Rob Botwright
Library of Congress Cataloging-in-Publication Data
ISBN 978-1-83938-752-4
Cover design by Rizzo

Disclaimer

The contents of this book are based on extensive research and the best available historical sources. However, the author and publisher make no claims, promises, or guarantees about the accuracy, completeness, or adequacy of the information contained herein. The information in this book is provided on an "as is" basis, and the author and publisher disclaim any and all liability for any errors, omissions, or inaccuracies in the information or for any actions taken in reliance on such information. The opinions and views expressed in this book are those of the author and do not necessarily reflect the official policy or position of any organization or individual mentioned in this book. Any reference to specific people, places, or events is intended only to provide historical context and is not intended to defame or malign any group, individual, or entity. The information in this book is intended for educational and entertainment purposes only. It is not intended to be a substitute for professional advice or judgment. Readers are encouraged to conduct their own research and to seek professional advice where appropriate. Every effort has been made to obtain necessary permissions and acknowledgments for all images and other copyrighted material used in this book. Any errors or omissions in this regard are unintentional, and the author and publisher will correct them in future editions.

BOOK 1 - DELPHI PASCAL PROGRAMMING ESSENTIALS: MASTERING EFFICIENT CODE EDITING

BOOK 1 - DELPHI PASCAL PROGRAMMING ESSENTIALS: MASTERING EFFICIENT CODE EDITING

BOOK 1 - DELPHI PASCAL PROGRAMMING ESSENTIALS: MASTERING EFFICIENT CODE EDITING

BOOK 1 - DELPHI PASCAL PROGRAMMING ESSENTIALS: MASTERING EFFICIENT CODE EDITING

Introduction

Welcome to the comprehensive book bundle "Delphi Pascal Programming: Efficient Code Editing, Visual Designing, and Integrated Debugging." This bundle is designed to provide developers of all levels with a comprehensive guide to mastering Delphi Pascal programming, covering essential techniques for efficient code editing, visual designing, and integrated debugging.

Book 1, "Delphi Pascal Programming Essentials: Mastering Efficient Code Editing," serves as the foundation for your journey into Delphi Pascal programming. Here, you will learn essential techniques and best practices for writing clean, maintainable code, leveraging powerful code editing features, and optimizing productivity with shortcuts and customizations.

Moving on to Book 2, "From Basics to Brilliance: Visual Designing in Delphi Pascal Programming," you will explore the world of visual design within the Delphi IDE. From layout and alignment strategies to integrating graphics and animations, this book empowers you to create visually stunning user interfaces that enhance user experience and engagement.

In Book 3, "Advanced Techniques in Delphi Pascal: Integrated Debugging Strategies," you will delve into the intricacies of debugging, learning advanced strategies for identifying, diagnosing, and resolving software defects. With a focus on integrated debugging tools and techniques within the Delphi IDE, you will learn how to effectively troubleshoot and debug complex applications, ensuring optimal performance and reliability.

Finally, Book 4, "Delphi Pascal Programming Pro: Fine-Tuning Code Editing and Visual Designing for Experts," caters to seasoned professionals seeking to refine their expertise in Delphi programming. Through advanced topics and expert-level insights, you will gain a deeper understanding of code editing, visual designing, and debugging, enabling you to tackle even the most challenging projects with confidence and precision.

Whether you are a novice developer looking to master the essentials or an experienced professional seeking to refine your expertise, "Delphi Pascal Programming" provides a comprehensive resource to help you achieve your goals and unlock your full potential in the world of software development. Let's embark on this journey together and elevate your Delphi Pascal programming skills to new heights.

BOOK 1
DELPHI PASCAL PROGRAMMING ESSENTIALS:
MASTERING EFFICIENT CODE EDITING

ROB BOTWRIGHT

Chapter 1: Introduction to Delphi Pascal Programming

Pascal, a high-level programming language created by Professor Niklaus Wirth in the late 1960s, remains a fundamental language in the realm of computer science and software development. It was designed with the primary goal of promoting structured programming practices, emphasizing clarity and reliability in code. Pascal gained popularity due to its simplicity and strict syntax rules, making it an excellent choice for teaching programming fundamentals to beginners and for developing robust, maintainable software applications. The language was named in honor of the French mathematician and philosopher Blaise Pascal, reflecting its roots in mathematics and logical reasoning.

One of the defining features of Pascal is its strong typing system, which enforces strict data type compatibility and helps prevent common programming errors. This emphasis on type safety contributes to the reliability and stability of Pascal programs, making them less prone to runtime errors and memory corruption issues. Pascal supports a wide range of built-in data types, including integers, real numbers, characters, booleans, and enumerated types, providing programmers with versatile tools for expressing various concepts and data structures.

Pascal programs are organized into modules known as units, each containing declarations, definitions, and procedures or functions that encapsulate specific functionality. This modular structure promotes code reusability and maintainability, allowing developers to divide their programs into manageable components and focus on individual tasks independently. Furthermore, Pascal supports procedural programming paradigms, enabling developers to define procedures and functions as reusable building blocks for implementing algorithms and logic.

In addition to procedural programming, Pascal also introduced the concept of structured programming, which emphasizes the use of control structures such as sequences, loops, and conditional statements to organize code flow in a clear and understandable manner. By enforcing structured programming principles, Pascal encourages developers to write well-organized, readable code that is easier to understand and maintain, even as projects grow in complexity.

Another notable aspect of Pascal is its support for recursion, a programming technique where a function calls itself to solve a problem by breaking it down into smaller subproblems. Recursion is a powerful tool for solving problems that exhibit a recursive structure, such as mathematical functions, tree traversal algorithms, and sorting algorithms like quicksort and mergesort. Pascal's support for recursion allows developers to implement elegant and efficient solutions to a wide range of problems, leveraging the language's simplicity and expressiveness.

Moreover, Pascal provides extensive support for file handling, allowing programmers to read from and write to external files for data storage and retrieval. This capability is essential for developing applications that need to persist data across sessions or communicate with external systems through file-based interfaces. Pascal's file handling features include built-in functions for opening, reading, writing, and closing files, as well as support for text and binary file formats.

Furthermore, Pascal's standard library includes a variety of utility functions and data structures that facilitate common programming tasks, such as string manipulation, mathematical operations, and dynamic memory allocation. These built-in features enhance the productivity of developers by providing them with a rich set of tools and resources for building efficient and reliable software applications.

Despite its age, Pascal continues to be relevant in modern software development, with several dialects and implementations available for different platforms and purposes. One of the most popular derivatives of Pascal is Delphi, a powerful integrated development environment (IDE) for rapid application development (RAD) that combines the flexibility of Pascal with modern GUI design tools and frameworks. Delphi enables developers to create cross-platform desktop, mobile, and web applications using the Object Pascal language, extending the legacy of Pascal into the digital age.

In summary, Pascal programming language offers a solid foundation for learning programming concepts and developing software applications. Its simplicity, clarity, and reliability make it an ideal choice for beginners and professionals alike, while its support for structured programming, strong typing, recursion, and file handling ensures versatility and efficiency in solving a wide range of problems. Pascal's legacy lives on in modern programming languages and development tools, reaffirming its status as a timeless classic in the world of computer programming.

Delphi, a highly influential integrated development environment (IDE), has significantly shaped the landscape of software development since its inception. Born out of Borland International's labs in the early 1990s, Delphi represented a groundbreaking shift in software development methodologies. Its genesis can be traced back to Turbo Pascal, a popular programming language developed by Anders Hejlsberg and Borland in the 1980s. Turbo Pascal gained widespread acclaim for its fast compilation speed, efficient code generation, and ease of use, establishing Borland as a leading force in the software industry.

The development of Delphi was driven by the need for a more comprehensive toolset that could empower developers to build robust, visually appealing applications for the burgeoning Windows platform. Borland's founder and CEO, Philippe Kahn, envisioned a revolutionary IDE that would combine the power of Turbo Pascal's compiler with advanced visual design tools and rapid application development (RAD) capabilities. This vision culminated in the release of Delphi 1.0 in 1995, marking the dawn of a new era in software development.

Delphi introduced a groundbreaking approach to software development, known as visual programming, which enabled developers to design user interfaces graphically using drag-and-drop components. This paradigm shift democratized software development, allowing developers of all skill levels to create professional-grade applications with unprecedented ease and efficiency. Delphi's innovative visual design tools, including the Form Designer and Object Inspector, provided developers with a visual representation of their applications' user interfaces, streamlining the development process and fostering creativity.

One of Delphi's most significant contributions to software development was the introduction of the Borland Component Library (VCL), a comprehensive set of reusable components and controls for building Windows applications. The VCL revolutionized the way developers approached application development by providing them with a rich palette of pre-built UI elements, data access components, and visual effects that could be easily customized and extended. This modular approach to software development accelerated development cycles and facilitated code reuse, resulting in more efficient and maintainable applications.

Delphi's success continued to grow with the release of subsequent versions, each introducing new features and enhancements that further solidified its position as a leading development platform. Delphi 2.0 introduced support for 32-bit Windows development, paving the way for more powerful and scalable applications. Delphi

3.0 introduced support for database connectivity through the Borland Database Engine (BDE), enabling developers to build data-driven applications with ease.

Delphi's evolution continued with the release of Delphi 4.0, which introduced the Integrated Development Environment (IDE) that featured a redesigned user interface and enhanced productivity tools. Delphi 5.0 introduced support for Component Object Model (COM) development, enabling developers to create COM objects and interact with external COM components seamlessly. Delphi 6.0 further expanded Delphi's capabilities with support for web development, allowing developers to build web applications using the IntraWeb framework.

In the early 2000s, Borland faced financial challenges and underwent a series of restructuring efforts that impacted the development and marketing of Delphi. Despite these challenges, Delphi continued to evolve under the stewardship of Borland and later Embarcadero Technologies, which acquired the Delphi product line in 2008. Embarcadero focused on modernizing Delphi and expanding its capabilities to meet the evolving needs of developers in an increasingly diverse and competitive market.

In recent years, Delphi has undergone a renaissance with the release of Delphi 10.0, which introduced support for cross-platform development targeting Windows, macOS, iOS, and Android. This cross-platform capability, made possible by the FireMonkey framework, has revitalized Delphi's relevance in the mobile and multi-device development space, enabling developers to leverage their existing Delphi skills to reach a broader audience across different platforms.

Today, Delphi remains a popular choice for developers seeking a versatile and productive development environment for building high-performance, visually stunning applications. Its rich history and legacy of innovation continue to inspire developers around the world, cementing its status as a timeless classic in the realm of software development. With its steadfast commitment to quality, innovation, and developer empowerment, Delphi is poised to shape the future of software development for years to come.

Chapter 2: Understanding the Delphi Integrated Development Environment (IDE)

Navigating the Delphi Integrated Development Environment (IDE) interface is a fundamental skill for developers seeking to harness the full power of this robust development environment. Upon launching Delphi, developers are greeted by a familiar workspace comprising various components and tools designed to streamline the software development process. At the heart of the Delphi IDE lies the main window, which serves as the central hub for accessing and managing project files, source code, and development tools. The main window is divided into several distinct areas, each serving a specific purpose in the software development workflow.

One of the primary components of the Delphi IDE interface is the Code Editor, where developers spend the majority of their time writing, editing, and debugging code. The Code Editor provides a feature-rich environment with syntax highlighting, code completion, and error checking capabilities, enabling developers to write code with speed and precision. To open the Code Editor, developers can either create a new source file or open an existing one using the File menu or the Ctrl + N and Ctrl + O keyboard shortcuts. Once the Code Editor is open, developers can begin writing code and exploring the various features and functionalities available.

Adjacent to the Code Editor is the Object Inspector, a powerful tool for visualizing and manipulating the properties of objects within the application. The Object Inspector displays a hierarchical view of the components and controls used in the application, allowing developers to inspect and modify their properties and event handlers with ease. To access the Object Inspector, developers can simply click on the desired component or control in the Form Designer or select it from the drop-down list at the top of the Object Inspector window. From there, developers can view and edit the properties of the selected object, such as its size, position, and appearance, as well as assign event handlers to respond to user interactions.

Another essential component of the Delphi IDE interface is the Form Designer, a visual layout tool for designing the user interface of applications. The Form Designer provides a WYSIWYG (What You See Is What You Get) environment where developers can drag and drop components onto a form to create the desired layout. To access the Form Designer, developers can either double-click on a form file in the Project Manager or select it from the View menu. Once in the Form Designer, developers can add and arrange components, set their properties, and define event handlers to create interactive and visually appealing user interfaces.

In addition to the Code Editor, Object Inspector, and Form Designer, the Delphi IDE interface also includes several other useful tools and panels to aid developers in their software development tasks. One such tool is the Tool Palette, which contains a collection of components and controls that can be added to forms and frames in the application. The Tool Palette is organized into categories such as Standard, Additional, and Data Access, making it easy for developers to find and select the desired components for their projects. To access the Tool Palette, developers can click on the View menu and select Tool Palette or use the Ctrl + Alt + P keyboard shortcut.

Another indispensable tool in the Delphi IDE interface is the Project Manager, which provides a hierarchical view of the project structure and allows developers to manage project files, folders, and dependencies. The Project Manager displays a tree-like structure of the project, with nodes representing units, forms, resources, and other project elements. Developers can expand and collapse nodes, rename files, and add new files to the project directly from the Project Manager window. To open the Project Manager, developers can click on the View menu and select Project Manager or use the Ctrl + Alt + F11 keyboard shortcut.

Additionally, the Delphi IDE interface includes several other panels and windows that can be docked, undocked, resized, and rearranged to suit the preferences of individual developers. These panels include the Message View, which displays compiler messages, warnings, and errors; the Structure View, which provides a hierarchical view of the current source file; and the Search Results window, which displays search results for text searches performed within the IDE. Developers can customize the layout of the IDE interface by dragging and dropping panels to different locations, resizing panels, and docking or undocking panels as needed.

In summary, navigating the Delphi IDE interface is a fundamental skill for developers seeking to maximize their productivity and efficiency in software development. By familiarizing themselves with the various components, tools, and panels available in the IDE, developers can streamline their workflow, write code with speed and precision, and create visually stunning applications with ease. With its intuitive interface and powerful features, the Delphi IDE continues to be the tool of choice for developers around the world, empowering them to bring their creative ideas to life and build innovative solutions for a wide range of platforms and industries.

Exploring IDE features and tool windows is essential for developers seeking to maximize their productivity and efficiency in software development. The integrated development environment (IDE) serves as the central hub for managing project files, writing and editing code, debugging applications, and deploying software solutions. Within the IDE, developers have access to a wide range of features and tools designed to streamline the development process and facilitate collaboration among team members. By familiarizing themselves with these features and tool windows, developers can leverage the full power of the IDE to create high-quality software solutions that meet the needs of their users.

One of the key features of the IDE is the Code Editor, where developers spend the majority of their time writing and editing code. The Code Editor provides a feature-rich environment with syntax highlighting, code completion, and error checking capabilities, enabling developers to write code with speed and precision. To open the Code Editor, developers can create a new source file or open an existing one using the File menu or the Ctrl + N and Ctrl + O keyboard shortcuts. Once the Code Editor is open, developers can begin writing code and exploring the various features and functionalities available.

Adjacent to the Code Editor is the Object Inspector, a powerful tool for visualizing and manipulating the properties of objects within the application. The Object Inspector displays a hierarchical view of the components and controls used in the application, allowing developers to inspect and modify their properties and event handlers with ease. To access the Object Inspector, developers can simply click on the desired component or control in the Form Designer or select it from the drop-down list at the top of the Object Inspector window. From there, developers can view and edit the properties of the selected object, such as its size, position, and appearance, as well as assign event handlers to respond to user interactions.

Another essential tool in the IDE is the Form Designer, a visual layout tool for designing the user interface of applications. The Form Designer provides a WYSIWYG (What You See Is What You Get) environment where developers can drag and drop components onto a form to create the desired layout. To access the Form Designer, developers can either double-click on a form file in the Project Manager or select it from the View menu. Once in the Form Designer, developers can add and arrange components, set their properties, and define event handlers to create interactive and visually appealing user interfaces.

In addition to the Code Editor, Object Inspector, and Form Designer, the IDE also includes several other useful tools and panels to aid developers in their software development tasks. One such tool is the Tool Palette, which contains a collection of components and controls that can be added to forms and frames in the application. The Tool Palette is organized into categories such as Standard, Additional, and Data Access, making it easy for developers to find and select the desired components for their projects. To access the Tool Palette, developers can click on the View menu and select Tool Palette or use the Ctrl + Alt + P keyboard shortcut.

Another indispensable tool in the IDE is the Project Manager, which provides a hierarchical view of the project structure and allows developers to manage project files, folders, and dependencies. The Project Manager displays a tree-like structure of the project, with nodes representing units, forms, resources, and other project elements. Developers can expand and collapse nodes, rename files, and add new files to the project directly from the Project Manager window. To open the Project Manager, developers can click on the View menu and select Project Manager or use the Ctrl + Alt + F11 keyboard shortcut.

Additionally, the IDE includes several other panels and windows that can be docked, undocked, resized, and rearranged to suit the preferences of individual developers. These panels include the Message View, which displays compiler messages, warnings, and errors; the Structure View, which provides a hierarchical view of the current source file; and the Search Results window, which displays search results for text searches performed within the IDE. Developers can customize the layout of the IDE interface by dragging and dropping panels to different locations, resizing panels, and docking or undocking panels as needed.

In summary, exploring IDE features and tool windows is essential for developers seeking to maximize their productivity and efficiency in software development. By familiarizing themselves with the various components, tools, and panels available in the IDE, developers can streamline their workflow, write code with speed and precision, and create visually stunning applications with ease. With its intuitive interface and powerful features, the IDE continues to be the tool of choice for developers around the world, empowering them to bring their creative ideas to life and build innovative solutions for a wide range of platforms and industries.

Chapter 3: Fundamentals of Pascal Language Syntax

Understanding the basic structure of Pascal programs is fundamental for anyone delving into this programming language, which has been revered for its simplicity and clarity since its inception in the late 1960s. At its core, a Pascal program comprises a series of declarations and statements organized within a structured framework. The structure of a Pascal program typically consists of several key elements, including program heading, program body, and program units.

The program heading serves as the entry point of a Pascal program and provides essential information about the program, such as its name and any parameters it may accept. The program heading begins with the **program** keyword followed by the name of the program, which serves as its identifier. For example, a simple Pascal program may start with:

Copy code

program HelloWorld;

Following the program heading is the program body, which encapsulates the main logic and functionality of the program. The program body is enclosed within a **begin...end** block and contains declarations, statements, and executable code. Declarations are used to define variables, constants, types, and other program elements that will be used throughout the program. Statements, on the other hand, are executable instructions that perform specific actions or operations.

The program body typically starts with the **begin** keyword and ends with the **end** keyword. For example: arduinoCopy code

begin // Program statements go here end.

Within the program body, developers can define various program units, such as functions, procedures, and blocks, to modularize and organize their code. Functions and procedures are reusable blocks of code that perform specific tasks and can accept parameters and return values. They are declared using the **function** and **procedure** keywords, respectively, followed by their names, parameters (if any), and return types (for functions). For example:

arduinoCopy code

procedure DisplayMessage; begin writeln('Hello, World!'); end;

Blocks, on the other hand, are used to group related statements and declarations within the program body. They are declared using the **begin...end** block and can be nested within other blocks to create a hierarchical structure. For example:

arduinoCopy code

begin // Outer block begin // Inner block end; end;

In addition to program units, Pascal programs may also include directives and comments to provide additional information and annotations. Directives are special instructions that modify the behavior of the compiler or control the compilation process. They are prefixed with the **{** and **}** characters and can be used to include or exclude specific sections of code, define compiler options, or provide documentation. For example:

phpCopy code

```
{$IFDEF DEBUG} // Debugging code goes here
{$ENDIF}
```

Comments, on the other hand, are used to add explanatory notes and annotations within the code to improve readability and maintainability. Comments are ignored by the compiler and have no effect on the execution of the program. Pascal supports two types of comments: single-line comments, denoted by the **//** characters, and multi-line comments, enclosed within **{** and **}** characters. For example:

arduinoCopy code

```
// This is a single-line comment { This is a multi-line comment }
```

Once the Pascal program has been written, it can be compiled and executed using a Pascal compiler. The compiler translates the human-readable source code into machine-readable instructions that can be executed by the computer. Pascal compilers typically provide a command-line interface (CLI) for compiling and running programs. For example, to compile a Pascal program named **HelloWorld.pas**, developers can use the following command:

Copy code

```
fpc HelloWorld.pas
```

This command invokes the Free Pascal Compiler (FPC) and compiles the **HelloWorld.pas** source file into an executable binary file. Once the program has been compiled successfully, developers can run it by executing the generated binary file. For example:

Copy code

```
./HelloWorld
```

This command runs the **HelloWorld** executable, which displays the output of the program to the console.

In summary, understanding the basic structure of Pascal programs is essential for developers seeking to write clear, concise, and maintainable code in this venerable programming language. By familiarizing themselves with the various elements of a Pascal program, including program headings, program bodies, program units, directives, and comments, developers can create well-structured and efficient programs that meet the needs of their users. Additionally, mastering the use of Pascal compilers and CLI commands enables developers to compile and run their programs with ease, bringing their creative ideas to life and building innovative solutions for a wide range of platforms and industries.

Syntax rules and conventions in Pascal play a crucial role in ensuring the clarity, readability, and maintainability of code written in this structured programming language. Pascal, renowned for its simplicity and strict adherence to syntax rules, follows a set of conventions that govern how code is written and structured. These rules dictate everything from naming conventions for identifiers to the placement of semicolons and parentheses, creating a consistent and uniform coding style across Pascal programs.

One of the fundamental syntax rules in Pascal is the use of semicolons to terminate statements. Semicolons serve as statement separators and are used to denote the end of one statement and the beginning of the next. For example:

scssCopy code

```
writeln ('Hello, World!'); writeln ('Welcome to Pascal programming!');
```

Here, the semicolon at the end of each writeln statement indicates the termination of the statement.

Another important syntax rule in Pascal is the use of reserved keywords to define language constructs such as variables, constants, types, procedures, and functions. These keywords are predefined and cannot be used as identifiers for variables or other program elements. Examples of reserved keywords in Pascal include program, begin, end, var, const, procedure, function, if, then, else, while, repeat, until, for, do, and case.

Pascal also follows strict rules for naming identifiers, such as variables, constants, types, procedures, and functions. Identifiers must begin with a letter and can contain letters, digits, and underscores. However, Pascal is case-insensitive, meaning that uppercase and lowercase letters are treated as equivalent. It is common practice to use meaningful and descriptive names for identifiers to enhance code readability and understandability. For example:

phpCopy code

```pascal
var num1, num2: integer; // Variable names num1 and
num2 PI: real = 3.14159; // Constant name PI
```

In Pascal, comments are used to add explanatory notes and annotations within the code, providing additional information to aid understanding. Comments are ignored by the compiler and have no effect on the execution of the program. Pascal supports two types of comments: single-line comments, denoted by the // characters, and multi-line comments, enclosed within { and } characters. For example:

arduinoCopy code

```pascal
// This is a single-line comment { This is a multi-line
comment }
```

Furthermore, Pascal uses parentheses to denote precedence and to group expressions. Parentheses are used to clarify the order of operations in arithmetic expressions and to control the flow of execution in conditional statements and function calls. For example:

cssCopy code

```pascal
result := (num1 + num2) * num3; // Use parentheses to
specify the order of operations
```

Additionally, Pascal uses indentation to visually organize and structure code blocks, making it easier to understand the flow of control in the program. Indentation is typically done using spaces or tabs and is used to indicate the beginning and end of code blocks, such as loops, conditional statements, and procedure bodies. For example:

arduinoCopy code

begin // Indentation indicates the beginning of a code block if num > 0 then begin // Nested code block writeln('Positive'); end; end;

Moreover, Pascal requires the use of explicit type declarations for variables and parameters, ensuring type safety and preventing type-related errors. Type declarations specify the data type of a variable or parameter and are declared using the colon (:) operator followed by the desired data type. For example:

phpCopy code

var age: integer; // Variable age with integer data type price: real; // Variable price with real data type name: string; // Variable name with string data type

Finally, Pascal follows specific formatting conventions for program structure, such as the placement of program headings, program bodies, and program units. Program headings typically begin with the program keyword followed by the name of the program, while program bodies are enclosed within begin...end blocks. Program units, such as functions and procedures, are defined using the function and procedure keywords, respectively, followed by their names, parameters, and return types.

Once a Pascal program has been written according to the syntax rules and conventions, it can be compiled and executed using a Pascal compiler. Pascal compilers typically provide a command-line interface (CLI) for compiling and running programs. For example, to compile a Pascal program named HelloWorld.pas, developers can use the following command:

Copy code

```
fpc HelloWorld.pas
```

This command invokes the Free Pascal Compiler (FPC) and compiles the HelloWorld.pas source file into an executable binary file. Once the program has been compiled successfully, developers can run it by executing the generated binary file. For example:

Copy code

```
./HelloWorld
```

This command runs the HelloWorld executable, which executes the Pascal program and displays the output to the console.

In summary, understanding syntax rules and conventions in Pascal is essential for writing clear, readable, and maintainable code in this structured programming language. By following these rules, developers can create well-structured and efficient programs that meet the needs of their users. Additionally, mastering the use of Pascal compilers and CLI commands enables developers to compile and run their programs with ease, bringing their creative ideas to life and building innovative solutions for a wide range of platforms and industries.

Chapter 4: Essential Code Editing Tools and Techniques

Text editing features in the Delphi Integrated Development Environment (IDE) are essential tools for developers seeking to write, edit, and manage code efficiently. The Delphi IDE provides a comprehensive set of text editing features designed to streamline the development process and enhance productivity. These features include syntax highlighting, code completion, code templates, code folding, and many others, all of which contribute to a seamless coding experience.

Syntax highlighting is one of the most basic yet crucial text editing features in the Delphi IDE. It enhances code readability by applying different colors and styles to various elements of the code, such as keywords, comments, strings, and identifiers. Syntax highlighting makes it easier for developers to distinguish between different parts of the code and quickly identify errors or inconsistencies. To enable syntax highlighting in the Delphi IDE, developers can navigate to the Editor Options dialog box and select the desired syntax highlighting scheme from the list of available options.

Code completion is another powerful text editing feature in the Delphi IDE that helps developers write code faster and with fewer errors. Code completion automatically suggests code snippets, keywords, variables, and function names as developers type, reducing the need for manual typing and minimizing typos. Code completion is triggered by pressing the Ctrl + Space keyboard shortcut or by typing the first few characters of the desired identifier. Developers can then select the desired suggestion from the list of available options and press Enter to insert it into the code.

Code templates are pre-defined code snippets that can be quickly inserted into the code using keyboard shortcuts or menu commands. Code templates are useful for common programming tasks, such as creating loops, conditional statements, or function declarations, and can help developers write code more efficiently. Delphi IDE provides a set of built-in code templates for various programming constructs, and developers can also create custom code templates to suit their specific needs. To insert a code template into the code, developers can use the Ctrl + J keyboard shortcut or select the desired template from the Code Templates menu.

Code folding is a text editing feature in the Delphi IDE that allows developers to collapse or expand blocks of code to focus on specific parts of the code. Code folding is particularly useful for navigating large code files and reducing visual clutter by hiding irrelevant or less important sections of the code. Delphi IDE supports code folding for various code constructs, including procedures, functions, conditional statements, and loops. To fold or unfold a code block, developers can click on the arrow icon next to the code block's header or use the Ctrl + Shift + Minus and Ctrl + Shift + Plus keyboard shortcuts.

Another useful text editing feature in the Delphi IDE is code navigation, which enables developers to quickly navigate between different parts of the code using keyboard shortcuts or menu commands. Code navigation features include Go To Definition, Go To Declaration, Find References, and Find Symbol, which allow developers to jump to the definition or declaration of a variable, function, or type, find all references to a specific identifier, or locate a symbol within the code file. These features help developers understand the structure and dependencies of the code and navigate it more efficiently.

In addition to these core text editing features, the Delphi IDE also provides several other tools and utilities to enhance the coding experience. These include code formatting, code refactoring, code analysis, and version control integration, among others. Code formatting tools automatically format the code according to predefined style rules, ensuring consistency and readability across the codebase. Code refactoring tools automate common code restructuring tasks, such as renaming variables, extracting methods, or moving code blocks, to improve code maintainability and organization.

Code analysis tools identify potential errors, warnings, or code smells in the code and provide suggestions for improvement. Version control integration allows developers to manage code changes, collaborate with team members, and track the history of code revisions using popular version control systems such as Git or Subversion. These tools and utilities, combined with the core text editing features, provide developers with a comprehensive set of tools for writing, editing, and managing code in the Delphi IDE.

Deploying these text editing features in the Delphi IDE is straightforward and does not require any additional configuration or setup. Developers can simply enable or disable the desired features from the Editor Options dialog box and customize their behavior according to their preferences. Additionally, developers can explore the various keyboard shortcuts and menu commands available for accessing these features and incorporate them into their coding workflow to improve efficiency and productivity.

In summary, text editing features in the Delphi IDE are essential tools for developers seeking to write, edit, and manage code efficiently. These features, including syntax highlighting, code completion, code templates, code folding, and many others, enhance code readability, streamline the development process, and improve productivity. By leveraging these features effectively and incorporating them into their coding workflow, developers can create high-quality software solutions with ease and confidence.

Utilizing code navigation and search tools is

paramount for developers striving to efficiently navigate, understand, and modify codebases of any size or complexity. In the modern software development landscape, where projects can span hundreds or thousands of files and contain millions of lines of code, having robust code navigation and search capabilities is essential for maintaining productivity and minimizing development time. Fortunately, most integrated development environments (IDEs) and text editors offer a wide range of features and tools designed to facilitate code navigation and searching, empowering developers to quickly locate and explore code elements, understand their dependencies, and make informed changes.

One of the fundamental code navigation tools available in many IDEs and text editors is the "Go To Definition" feature. This feature allows developers to quickly navigate to the declaration or definition of a specific identifier, such as a variable, function, class, or method, within the codebase. By simply positioning the cursor over the identifier and invoking the appropriate keyboard shortcut or menu command, developers can instantly jump to the corresponding definition, enabling them to understand how the identifier is defined and used throughout the codebase.

Similarly, the "Go To Declaration" feature complements the "Go To Definition" feature by allowing developers to navigate from a usage of an identifier to its declaration or definition. This feature is particularly useful when working with functions, methods, or classes, as it enables developers to quickly understand the signature and implementation of the identifier being used. By seamlessly traversing between declarations and usages, developers can gain a comprehensive understanding of the code structure and its dependencies, facilitating more efficient code exploration and modification.

Another invaluable code navigation tool is the "Find References" feature, which allows developers to quickly locate all references to a specific identifier within the codebase. By selecting the identifier and invoking the appropriate command, developers can generate a list of all occurrences of the identifier throughout the project, including its declarations, usages, and invocations. This feature is invaluable for understanding the impact of changes to a particular identifier and identifying potential areas of code that may be affected by those changes.

Furthermore, IDEs and text editors often provide powerful search capabilities that enable developers to perform complex searches and filters within the codebase. For example, developers can search for specific text patterns, regular expressions, or code elements using advanced search tools, such as the "Find in Files" or "Search Everywhere" features. These tools allow developers to quickly locate relevant code snippets, files, or symbols within the project, even in large and complex codebases.

Additionally, IDEs and text editors may offer code navigation features tailored to specific programming languages or frameworks. For example, in object-oriented programming languages like Java or C#, IDEs often provide features such as "Go To Type Hierarchy" or "Go To Implementation," which allow developers to navigate between base classes, derived classes, and interface implementations. Similarly, in web development frameworks like React or Angular, IDEs may offer features such as "Go To Component Definition" or "Go To Template," which facilitate navigation between component files, templates, and stylesheets.

Deploying these code navigation and search tools in IDEs and text editors is straightforward and typically involves accessing the corresponding features through keyboard shortcuts or menu commands. For example, in many IDEs, developers can use the Ctrl + Click keyboard shortcut or right-click context menu to navigate to definitions or declarations of identifiers. Similarly, they can use the Ctrl + Shift + F keyboard shortcut or the "Find in Files" menu command to perform a global search within the codebase. Additionally, developers can customize the behavior and preferences of these tools through the IDE's settings or preferences menu, allowing them to tailor the experience to their specific needs and preferences.

In summary, utilizing code navigation and search tools is essential for developers seeking to efficiently navigate, understand, and modify codebases of any size or complexity. By leveraging features such as "Go To Definition," "Go To Declaration," "Find References," and advanced search capabilities, developers can quickly locate and explore code elements, understand their dependencies, and make informed changes. These tools empower developers to maintain productivity, minimize development time, and deliver high-quality software solutions with confidence.

Chapter 5: Working with Variables and Data Types

Declaring and initializing variables is a fundamental aspect of programming in virtually every programming language, including Delphi. Variables serve as containers for storing data, and understanding how to declare and initialize them correctly is essential for writing clear, efficient, and maintainable code. In Delphi, variables must be declared before they can be used, and they can be initialized with an initial value if desired. The process of declaring and initializing variables involves specifying the variable's name, data type, and, optionally, its initial value.

In Delphi, variable declaration follows a specific syntax, which begins with the var keyword followed by a comma-separated list of variable declarations. Each variable declaration consists of the variable's name, followed by a colon (:), and then the variable's data type. For example, to declare an integer variable named num, we would use the following syntax:

delphiCopy code

```
var num: Integer;
```

This declares a variable named num of type Integer. Delphi supports a wide range of data types, including integers, floating-point numbers, characters, strings, booleans, and more. Developers can choose the appropriate data type based on the nature of the data they intend to store in the variable.

In addition to declaring variables, developers can also initialize them with an initial value at the time of declaration. Initializing variables ensures that they start with a known value, which can be useful for preventing undefined behavior and making the code more readable. To initialize a variable, developers can simply assign a value to it using the assignment operator (:=). For example, to declare and initialize an integer variable named count with an initial value of 0, we would use the following syntax:

delphiCopy code

```
var count: Integer; begin count := 0; end;
```

This declares a variable named count of type Integer and initializes it with the value 0. Similarly, variables can be initialized with other values, such as strings, floating-point numbers, or boolean values, depending on their data type.

Delphi also supports constant variables, which are variables whose values cannot be changed once they are initialized. Constant variables are declared using the const keyword instead of var, and they must be initialized with a value at the time of declaration. For example, to declare a constant integer variable named MAX_COUNT with an initial value of 100, we would use the following syntax:

delphiCopy code

```
const MAX_COUNT: Integer = 100;
```

This declares a constant variable named MAX_COUNT of type Integer and initializes it with the value 100. Constant variables are useful for defining values that are not expected to change throughout the execution of the program, such as mathematical constants or configuration settings.

In addition to single-variable declarations, Delphi also supports declaring multiple variables of the same data type in a single statement. This can be done by separating each variable declaration with a comma. For example, to declare three integer variables named x, y, and z, we would use the following syntax:

delphiCopy code

```
var x, y, z: Integer;
```

This declares three variables named x, y, and z of type Integer. Multiple-variable declarations can help improve code readability and reduce redundancy, especially when declaring variables of the same data type.

Furthermore, Delphi allows developers to declare variables within different scopes, such as global scope, procedure scope, or function scope. Variables declared within a procedure or function are only accessible within that procedure or function and are automatically deallocated when the procedure or function exits. Global variables, on the other hand, are accessible from anywhere within the program and persist for the duration of the program's execution. To declare a global variable, developers can declare it outside of any procedure or function, typically at the beginning of the program file.

Delphi also provides support for user-defined data types, such as records, arrays, and enumerated types, which can be used to group related data elements together. Records allow developers to define custom data structures consisting of multiple fields, each with its own data type. Arrays enable developers to create collections of homogeneous data elements indexed by an integer or enumerated value. Enumerated types allow developers to define a set of named constants with underlying integer values, making the code more readable and maintainable.

To summarize, declaring and initializing variables is a fundamental aspect of programming in Delphi. Variables serve as containers for storing data, and they must be declared before they can be used. Delphi provides a wide range of data types and supports declaring variables within different scopes. Additionally, variables can be initialized with an initial value at the time of declaration, and Delphi also supports constant variables, multiple-variable declarations, and user-defined data types. By understanding how to declare and initialize variables correctly, developers can write clear, efficient, and maintainable code in Delphi, making the most of this powerful programming language.

Exploring different data types in Pascal is essential for understanding how to represent and manipulate various types of data within a program. Pascal, like many programming languages, provides a rich set of built-in data types, each designed to serve specific purposes and accommodate different kinds of data. By leveraging the diverse range of data types available in Pascal, developers can write more expressive, efficient, and reliable code that meets the requirements of their applications.

One of the most basic data types in Pascal is the integer type, which represents whole numbers without any fractional or decimal part. Integer values can be positive, negative, or zero and are typically used to represent counts, indices, and other discrete quantities in a program. Pascal provides several variants of the integer type, including Byte, ShortInt, Word, SmallInt, LongInt, and Int64, each with its own range of values. For example, to declare an integer variable named num, we would use the following syntax:

pascalCopy code

```pascal
var num: Integer;
```

This declares a variable named num of type Integer, capable of holding integer values within a specific range defined by the platform's architecture.

In addition to integers, Pascal also supports floating-point data types, which represent numbers with fractional or decimal parts. Floating-point values are typically used to represent real numbers, such as measurements, temperatures, and monetary values, that require precision beyond what integers can provide. Pascal provides two floating-point data types: Single and Double, which represent single-precision and double-precision floating-point numbers, respectively. For example, to declare a floating-point variable named price, we would use the following syntax:

pascalCopy code

```pascal
var price: Double;
```

This declares a variable named price of type Double, capable of holding floating-point values with double precision.

Furthermore, Pascal supports character data types, which represent individual characters from the ASCII or Unicode character sets. Character values are enclosed within single quotes (') and can include letters, digits, symbols, and whitespace characters. Pascal provides two character data types: Char, which represents a single character, and String, which represents a sequence of characters. For example, to declare a character variable named letter, we would use the following syntax:

pascalCopy code

```pascal
var letter: Char;
```

This declares a variable named letter of type Char, capable of holding a single character value.

Pascal also includes boolean data types, which represent logical values indicating true or false. Boolean values are commonly used to control the flow of execution in conditional statements and loop constructs. Pascal provides a built-in boolean data type named Boolean, which has two possible values: True and False. For example, to declare a boolean variable named isValid, we would use the following syntax:

pascalCopy code

```pascal
var isValid: Boolean;
```

This declares a variable named isValid of type Boolean, capable of holding a boolean value indicating whether a condition is true or false.

Moreover, Pascal supports pointer data types, which store memory addresses that point to other variables or data structures in memory. Pointers are used to implement dynamic memory allocation, data structures like linked lists and trees, and low-level programming tasks such as interfacing with hardware devices. Pascal provides a built-in pointer data type named Pointer, which can point to variables of any data type. For example, to declare a pointer variable named ptr, we would use the following syntax:

pascalCopy code

```pascal
var ptr: Pointer;
```

This declares a variable named ptr of type Pointer, capable of holding memory addresses.

Additionally, Pascal allows developers to define custom data types using record, array, and enumerated types. Records are composite data types that group together related fields or members under a single name. Array types represent collections of elements of the same data type, indexed by an integer or enumerated value. Enumerated types define a set of named constants with underlying integer values, providing a more expressive way to represent categorical data. For example, to define an enumerated type named DayOfWeek, we would use the following syntax:

pascalCopy code

```pascal
type DayOfWeek = (Sunday, Monday, Tuesday, Wednesday, Thursday, Friday, Saturday);
```

This defines an enumerated type named DayOfWeek with seven named constants representing the days of the week.

In summary, exploring different data types in Pascal is crucial for understanding how to represent and manipulate data within a program. Pascal provides a diverse range of built-in data types, including integers, floating-point numbers, characters, booleans, and pointers, each tailored to specific needs and use cases. Additionally, Pascal allows developers to define custom data types using records, arrays, and enumerated types, providing flexibility and expressiveness in representing complex data structures. By leveraging the rich set of data types available in Pascal, developers can write more expressive, efficient, and reliable code that meets the requirements of their applications.

Chapter 6: Control Structures and Flow of Execution

Understanding conditional statements is fundamental to writing effective and logic-driven code in any programming language, including Pascal. Conditional statements allow developers to control the flow of execution in a program based on certain conditions or criteria, enabling them to create dynamic and responsive applications. In Pascal, conditional statements come in several forms, including the if statement, the if-else statement, the case statement, and the repeat-until statement. Each of these statements serves a specific purpose and can be used to implement various logic and decision-making scenarios within a program.

The if statement is perhaps the most basic form of a conditional statement in Pascal. It allows developers to execute a block of code only if a specified condition is true. The syntax of the if statement is straightforward: it begins with the if keyword followed by the condition to be evaluated, enclosed within parentheses, and then the code block to be executed if the condition is true, enclosed within begin and end keywords. For example:

pascalCopy code

```
if x > 0 then begin // Code to execute if x is greater than 0 end;
```

In this example, the code block inside the if statement will only execute if the condition x > 0 evaluates to true.

The if-else statement extends the functionality of the if statement by allowing developers to specify an alternative code block to execute if the condition is false. The syntax of the if-else statement consists of the if keyword followed by the condition, the code block to execute if the condition is true, the else keyword, and then the alternative code block to execute if the condition is false. For example:

pascalCopy code

if x > 0 then begin // Code to execute if x is greater than 0 end else begin // Code to execute if x is less than or equal to 0 end;

In this example, if the condition x > 0 is true, the code block inside the first begin and end will execute; otherwise, the code block inside the second begin and end will execute.

The case statement provides an alternative way to implement conditional logic based on the value of a variable or expression. It allows developers to specify a set of possible values or ranges and execute different code blocks depending on the value of the variable. The syntax of the case statement consists of the case keyword followed by the variable or expression to evaluate, the of keyword, and then a series of case labels specifying the values or ranges to match, each followed by a code block to execute. For example:

pascalCopy code

```
case dayOfWeek of Monday: begin // Code to execute if dayOfWeek is Monday end; Tuesday, Wednesday, Thursday: begin // Code to execute if dayOfWeek is Tuesday, Wednesday, or Thursday end; Friday..Saturday: begin // Code to execute if dayOfWeek is Friday or Saturday end; end;
```

In this example, the code block executed depends on the value of the dayOfWeek variable.

The repeat-until statement is a looping construct in Pascal that allows developers to repeat a block of code until a specified condition is true. Unlike the while loop, which evaluates the condition before executing the code block, the repeat-until loop evaluates the condition after executing the code block, ensuring that the code block is executed at least once. The syntax of the repeat-until statement consists of the repeat keyword followed by the code block to execute, the until keyword, and then the condition to evaluate. For example:

pascalCopy code

```
repeat // Code to execute until x > 10;
```

In this example, the code block will repeat until the condition $x > 10$ is true.

Conditional statements are commonly used in various programming tasks, such as input validation, error handling, and controlling program flow based on user input or system state. They allow developers to implement complex logic and decision-making scenarios within their programs, making them more flexible and responsive to different situations.

To deploy conditional statements in a Pascal program, developers can simply write the desired code blocks using the appropriate syntax within their program files. Once the code is written, they can compile the program using a Pascal compiler to generate an executable file. Pascal compilers typically provide a command-line interface (CLI) for compiling and running programs. For example, to compile a Pascal program named myProgram.pas, developers can use the following command:

bashCopy code

```
fpc myProgram.pas
```

This command invokes the Free Pascal Compiler (FPC) and compiles the myProgram.pas source file into an executable binary file. Once the program has been compiled successfully, developers can run it by executing the generated binary file. For example:

bashCopy code

```
./myProgram
```

This command runs the myProgram executable, which executes the Pascal program and displays the output to the console.

In summary, understanding conditional statements is essential for writing effective and logic-driven code in Pascal. By leveraging conditional statements such as the if statement, the if-else statement, the case statement, and the repeat-until statement, developers can implement complex logic and decision-making scenarios within their programs. These statements allow developers to control the flow of execution based on specific conditions or criteria, making their programs more dynamic and responsive. Deploying conditional statements in a Pascal program is straightforward and involves writing the desired code blocks using the appropriate syntax and compiling the program using a Pascal compiler.

Implementing loops in Pascal programs is fundamental to creating efficient and flexible code that can perform repetitive tasks with ease. Loops allow developers to iterate over collections of data, execute code multiple times, and control the flow of execution based on certain conditions. In Pascal, there are several types of loops available, including the for loop, the while loop, and the repeat-until loop, each serving a specific purpose and offering unique advantages for different programming scenarios.

The for loop is one of the most commonly used loop constructs in Pascal and is ideal for iterating over a sequence of values or performing a predetermined number of iterations. The syntax of the for loop consists of the for keyword followed by a loop variable, a starting value, an ending value, and an optional step value, separated by the to or downto keyword. For example:

pascalCopy code

```
for i := 1 to 10 do begin // Code to execute end;
```

In this example, the for loop iterates over the values of the loop variable i from 1 to 10, executing the code block inside the loop for each iteration.

The while loop is another commonly used loop construct in Pascal and is ideal for executing a block of code repeatedly as long as a specified condition is true. The syntax of the while loop consists of the while keyword followed by a condition to evaluate and then the code block to execute, enclosed within begin and end keywords. For example:

pascalCopy code

```
while x < 10 do begin // Code to execute end;
```

In this example, the while loop executes the code block inside it repeatedly as long as the condition x < 10 is true.

The repeat-until loop is similar to the while loop but evaluates the condition after executing the code block, ensuring that the code block is executed at least once. The syntax of the repeat-until loop consists of the repeat keyword followed by the code block to execute and then the until keyword followed by the condition to evaluate. For example:

pascalCopy code

```
repeat // Code to execute until x >= 10;
```

In this example, the repeat-until loop executes the code block inside it repeatedly until the condition x >= 10 is true.

Loops are commonly used in a wide range of programming tasks, such as iterating over arrays, processing lists, and implementing algorithms. They provide a convenient and efficient way to perform repetitive tasks and automate processes in a program. To deploy loops in a Pascal program, developers can simply write the desired loop constructs using the appropriate syntax within their program files. Once the code is written, they can compile the program using a Pascal compiler to generate an executable file. Pascal compilers typically provide a command-line interface (CLI) for compiling and running programs. For example, to compile a Pascal program named myProgram.pas, developers can use the following command:

bashCopy code

```
fpc myProgram.pas
```

This command invokes the Free Pascal Compiler (FPC) and compiles the myProgram.pas source file into an executable binary file. Once the program has been compiled successfully, developers can run it by executing the generated binary file. For example:

bashCopy code

```
./myProgram
```

This command runs the myProgram executable, which executes the Pascal program and displays the output to the console.

In summary, implementing loops in Pascal programs is essential for creating efficient and flexible code that can perform repetitive tasks with ease. By leveraging loop constructs such as the for loop, the while loop, and the repeat-until loop, developers can iterate over collections of data, execute code multiple times, and control the flow of execution based on certain conditions. Deploying loops in a Pascal program is straightforward and involves writing the desired loop constructs using the appropriate syntax and compiling the program using a Pascal compiler.

Chapter 7: Procedures and Functions in Pascal

Declaring and defining procedures in Pascal is fundamental to writing modular and reusable code that can be organized into smaller, manageable units. Procedures allow developers to encapsulate a sequence of instructions into a single named block, which can then be called and executed from different parts of a program. In Pascal, procedures are defined using the procedure keyword, followed by the procedure name, a list of parameters (if any), and then the procedure body, which contains the code to be executed when the procedure is called. The process of declaring and defining procedures involves specifying their names, parameter lists, return types (if any), and the code to be executed within them.

To declare a procedure in Pascal, developers use the procedure keyword followed by the name of the procedure and an optional list of parameters enclosed in parentheses. Parameters are variables that are used to pass data into or out of the procedure and can be of any data type supported by Pascal. For example:

pascalCopy code

procedure PrintMessage(message: string); begin // Code to execute end;

In this example, we declare a procedure named PrintMessage that takes a single parameter message of type string.

To define the procedure, developers provide the implementation of the procedure body, which contains the actual code to be executed when the procedure is called. This is done by writing the sequence of instructions within the procedure body enclosed between the begin and end keywords. For example:

pascalCopy code

```pascal
procedure PrintMessage(message: string); begin writeln(message); end;
```

In this example, the procedure body contains a single instruction to write the value of the message parameter to the standard output.

Procedures can also have multiple parameters, allowing developers to pass in multiple pieces of data for processing. Parameters are separated by commas within the parameter list. For example:

pascalCopy code

```pascal
procedure Swap(var x, y: Integer); var temp: Integer; begin temp := x; x := y; y := temp; end;
```

In this example, we define a procedure named Swap that takes two parameters x and y by reference (using the var keyword), allowing their values to be modified within the procedure.

Furthermore, procedures can have return values, allowing them to compute and return a result to the calling code. To specify a return type for a procedure, developers use the function keyword instead of procedure and specify the return type after the procedure name. For example:

pascalCopy code

```pascal
function Add(x, y: Integer): Integer; begin Result := x + y; end;
```

In this example, we define a function named Add that takes two parameters x and y and returns their sum as an Integer value.

Once procedures have been declared and defined, they can be called and executed from different parts of the program by using their names and providing the necessary arguments (if any). To call a procedure, developers simply write its name followed by the arguments (if any) enclosed in parentheses. For example:

pascalCopy code

```pascal
PrintMessage('Hello, world!');
```

This command calls the PrintMessage procedure and passes the string 'Hello, world!' as an argument.

To deploy procedures in a Pascal program, developers simply write the procedure declarations and definitions within their program files. Once the code is written, they can compile the program using a Pascal compiler to generate an executable file. Pascal compilers typically provide a command-line interface (CLI) for compiling and running programs. For example, to compile a Pascal program named myProgram.pas, developers can use the following command:

bashCopy code

```
fpc myProgram.pas
```

This command invokes the Free Pascal Compiler (FPC) and compiles the myProgram.pas source file into an executable binary file. Once the program has been compiled successfully, developers can run it by executing the generated binary file. For example:

bashCopy code

```
./myProgram
```

This command runs the myProgram executable, which executes the Pascal program and displays the output to the console.

In summary, declaring and defining procedures in Pascal is essential for writing modular and reusable code that can be organized into smaller, manageable units. Procedures allow developers to encapsulate a sequence of instructions into a single named block, which can then be called and executed from different parts of a program. By understanding how to declare, define, and call procedures in Pascal, developers can write more modular, organized, and maintainable code, making their programs easier to understand, debug, and extend. Deploying procedures in a Pascal program is straightforward and involves writing the necessary procedure declarations and definitions within the program files and compiling the program using a Pascal compiler.

Implementing functions for reusable code is a crucial aspect of programming in any language, including Pascal. Functions allow developers to encapsulate a specific task or computation into a named block of code that can be called from different parts of a program. In Pascal, functions are similar to procedures but with the added capability of returning a value to the caller. This makes functions particularly useful for performing calculations, data processing, and other operations that produce a result. To implement functions in Pascal, developers use the function keyword followed by the function name, a list of parameters (if any), the return type, and then the function body containing the code to be executed. The process involves declaring, defining, and calling functions within a Pascal program to encapsulate reusable logic and promote code modularity and maintainability.

To declare a function in Pascal, developers use the function keyword followed by the function name, a list of parameters (if any), the return type, and a semicolon. Parameters are optional and allow developers to pass data into the function for processing. The return type specifies the type of value that the function will return to the caller. For example:

pascalCopy code

```
function Add(x, y: Integer): Integer;
```

In this example, we declare a function named Add that takes two parameters x and y of type Integer and returns an Integer value.

Next, we define the function by providing its implementation within the function body. This is done by writing the sequence of instructions within the function body enclosed between the begin and end keywords. For example:

pascalCopy code

```
function Add(x, y: Integer): Integer; begin Result := x + y; end;
```

In this example, the function body contains a single instruction to return the sum of the parameters x and y as the result.

Once the function has been declared and defined, it can be called and executed from different parts of the program by using its name and providing the necessary arguments (if any). To call a function, developers simply write its name followed by the arguments (if any) enclosed in parentheses. For example:

pascalCopy code

```
sum := Add(3, 5);
```

In this example, the Add function is called with arguments 3 and 5, and the result is assigned to the variable sum.

Functions can also have multiple parameters, allowing developers to pass in multiple pieces of data for processing. Parameters are separated by commas within the parameter list. For example:

pascalCopy code

```pascal
function Multiply(x, y: Integer): Integer; begin Result := x * y; end;
```

In this example, we define a function named Multiply that takes two parameters x and y and returns their product as an Integer value.

Furthermore, functions can have various return types, including integers, floating-point numbers, characters, strings, booleans, and custom data types such as records and arrays. This allows developers to create functions that perform different types of calculations and operations and return the appropriate result. For example:

pascalCopy code

```pascal
function IsEven(num: Integer): Boolean; begin Result := (num mod 2 = 0); end;
```

In this example, we define a function named IsEven that takes a single parameter num of type Integer and returns a Boolean value indicating whether the number is even or not.

Implementing functions for reusable code is beneficial for promoting code modularity and maintainability in Pascal programs. By encapsulating specific tasks or computations into named blocks of code, developers can easily reuse the same logic in multiple parts of their program without duplicating code. This not only reduces redundancy but also makes the code easier to understand, debug, and maintain.

To deploy functions in a Pascal program, developers simply write the function declarations and definitions within their program files. Once the code is written, they can compile the program using a Pascal compiler to generate an executable file. Pascal compilers typically provide a command-line interface (CLI) for compiling and running programs. For example, to compile a Pascal program named myProgram.pas, developers can use the following command:

bashCopy code

```
fpc myProgram.pas
```

This command invokes the Free Pascal Compiler (FPC) and compiles the myProgram.pas source file into an executable binary file. Once the program has been compiled successfully, developers can run it by executing the generated binary file. For example:

bashCopy code

```
./myProgram
```

This command runs the myProgram executable, which executes the Pascal program and displays the output to the console.

In summary, implementing functions for reusable code is a fundamental aspect of programming in Pascal. Functions allow developers to encapsulate specific tasks or computations into named blocks of code that can be called and executed from different parts of a program. By understanding how to declare, define, and call functions in Pascal, developers can write more modular, organized, and maintainable code, making their programs easier to understand, debug, and extend. Deploying functions in a Pascal program is straightforward and involves writing the necessary function declarations and definitions within the program files and compiling the program using a Pascal compiler.

Chapter 8: Managing Input and Output Operations

Reading input from users is a fundamental aspect of programming, allowing applications to interact with users and respond dynamically to their input. In Pascal, reading user input typically involves using the ReadLn procedure, which reads a line of text from the standard input (usually the keyboard) and stores it in a variable. Additionally, the Read procedure can be used to read individual values of specific data types from the standard input. These techniques enable developers to create interactive programs that prompt users for input, process their responses, and provide appropriate feedback.

To read a line of text input from the user in Pascal, developers use the ReadLn procedure followed by the variable where the input will be stored. For example:

pascalCopy code

```
var userInput: string; begin ReadLn(userInput); end.
```

In this example, the ReadLn procedure reads a line of text input from the user and stores it in the userInput variable.

Similarly, to read individual values of specific data types from the user, developers can use the Read procedure followed by the variable(s) where the input will be stored. For example:

pascalCopy code

```
var userNumber: Integer; begin Read(userNumber); end.
```

In this example, the Read procedure reads an integer input from the user and stores it in the userNumber variable.

It's important to note that after reading input from the user, the program may need to perform additional processing or validation to ensure that the input is valid and meets the requirements of the application. For example, developers may need to check whether the input is within a certain range, is of the correct data type, or meets specific criteria before proceeding with further execution.

To deploy the technique of reading input from users in a Pascal program, developers simply write the necessary code to prompt for input, use the appropriate input reading procedures (ReadLn or Read), and store the input in variables for further processing. Once the code is written, they can compile the program using a Pascal compiler to generate an executable file. Pascal compilers typically provide a command-line Interface (CLI) for compiling and running programs. For example, to compile a Pascal program named myProgram.pas, developers can use the following command:

bashCopy code

```
fpc myProgram.pas
```

This command invokes the Free Pascal Compiler (FPC) and compiles the myProgram.pas source file into an executable binary file. Once the program has been compiled successfully, developers can run it by executing the generated binary file. For example:

bashCopy code

```
./myProgram
```

This command runs the myProgram executable, which executes the Pascal program and prompts the user for input.

Reading input from users is essential for creating interactive applications that can respond dynamically to user input. By leveraging input reading techniques in Pascal, developers can create programs that prompt users for input, process their responses, and provide appropriate feedback, making their applications more interactive and user-friendly.

Writing output to the console and files is a crucial aspect of programming, allowing developers to communicate information, display results, and save data for later use. In Pascal, output can be directed to the standard output (usually the console) using the Write and WriteLn procedures, which display text and values respectively. Additionally, output can be redirected to files using file handling procedures such as Assign, Rewrite, and Write to create, open, and write to files. These techniques enable developers to create applications that generate informative output, display results to users, and save data for persistence or further processing.

To write text or values to the console in Pascal, developers use the Write and WriteLn procedures followed by the text or values to be displayed. For example:

pascalCopy code

```
WriteLn('Hello, world!');
```

In this example, the WriteLn procedure displays the text "Hello, world!" followed by a newline character to the console.

Similarly, to display values to the console, developers can use the Write procedure followed by the values to be displayed. For example:

pascalCopy code

var num: Integer; begin num := 42; Write('The answer is: '); WriteLn(num); end.

In this example, the Write procedure displays the text "The answer is: " followed by the value of the num variable to the console.

To redirect output to a file in Pascal, developers first need to create or open a file using the Assign and Rewrite procedures. The Assign procedure associates a file variable with a file name, while the Rewrite procedure creates a new file or truncates an existing file for writing. For example:

pascalCopy code

var outputFile: TextFile; begin Assign(outputFile, 'output.txt'); Rewrite(outputFile); end.

In this example, we associate the outputFile variable with a file named "output.txt" and create or truncate the file for writing.

Once the file has been opened, developers can use the Write and WriteLn procedures to write text or values to the file. For example:

pascalCopy code

var outputFile: TextFile; begin Assign(outputFile, 'output.txt'); Rewrite(outputFile); WriteLn(outputFile, 'Hello, world!'); Close(outputFile); end.

In this example, the WriteLn procedure writes the text "Hello, world!" followed by a newline character to the file associated with the outputFile variable.

To deploy the technique of writing output to the console and files in a Pascal program, developers simply write the necessary code to display output using the Write and WriteLn procedures for the console, and use file handling procedures such as Assign, Rewrite, and Write to redirect output to files. Once the code is written, they can compile the program using a Pascal compiler to generate an executable file. Pascal compilers typically provide a command-line interface (CLI) for compiling and running programs. For example, to compile a Pascal program named myProgram.pas, developers can use the following command:

bashCopy code

fpc myProgram.pas

This command invokes the Free Pascal Compiler (FPC) and compiles the myProgram.pas source file into an executable binary file. Once the program has been compiled successfully, developers can run it by executing the generated binary file. For example:

bashCopy code

./myProgram

This command runs the myProgram executable, which executes the Pascal program and displays output to the console or writes output to files as specified in the program code.

Writing output to the console and files is essential for creating informative and interactive applications in Pascal. By leveraging output writing techniques, developers can communicate information, display results, and save data for persistence or further processing, making their applications more versatile and useful.

Chapter 9: Error Handling and Debugging Strategies

Identifying and handling runtime errors is an essential skill for programmers, as it allows them to diagnose and resolve issues that occur during the execution of their code. In Pascal, runtime errors can occur due to various reasons, such as division by zero, array bounds violations, invalid type conversions, and memory allocation failures. Identifying these errors involves understanding their causes and using debugging tools and techniques to locate the source of the problem. Once identified, runtime errors can be handled using error handling mechanisms such as exception handling and defensive programming strategies to gracefully handle unexpected situations and prevent program crashes.

When a runtime error occurs in a Pascal program, the compiler generates an error message indicating the nature of the error and its location in the code. These error messages provide valuable information that can help developers identify and diagnose the underlying issue. For example, if a division by zero error occurs, the compiler might output a message like "Runtime error 200: Division by zero" along with the line number where the error occurred.

To identify and diagnose runtime errors in a Pascal program, developers can use debugging tools and techniques such as logging, breakpoints, and stack traces. Logging involves inserting debug messages into the code to track the flow of execution and monitor the values of variables at different points in the program. Breakpoints allow developers to pause the execution of the program at specific points and inspect the state of the program's variables and data structures. Stack traces provide a detailed report of the sequence of function calls leading up to the error, helping developers trace the path of execution and locate the source of the problem.

Once a runtime error has been identified, developers can handle it using error handling mechanisms such as exception handling and defensive programming strategies. Exception handling involves using try-catch blocks to catch and handle exceptions that occur during the execution of the program. In Pascal, exceptions are objects that represent errors or unexpected conditions that disrupt the normal flow of execution. By enclosing potentially error-prone code within try-catch blocks, developers can gracefully handle exceptions and prevent program crashes.

pascalCopy code

```
try // Code that may cause a runtime error except // Handle the exception end;
```

In this example, the code within the try block is executed, and if a runtime error occurs, it is caught by the except block, where it can be handled appropriately.

Defensive programming strategies involve anticipating potential errors and taking proactive measures to prevent them from occurring. This may include adding input validation checks to ensure that user input is within acceptable ranges, using error-checking functions to verify the validity of data before processing it, and implementing fallback mechanisms to handle unexpected situations gracefully.

To deploy the technique of identifying and handling runtime errors in a Pascal program, developers can use debugging tools and techniques to diagnose errors, such as logging, breakpoints, and stack traces. Once the error has been identified, they can use error handling mechanisms such as exception handling and defensive programming strategies to handle the error gracefully and prevent program crashes. After implementing these measures, developers can test the program to ensure that it functions correctly under various conditions and handles runtime errors effectively.

Identifying and handling runtime errors is a critical aspect of software development, as it allows developers to create robust and reliable applications that can withstand unexpected conditions and provide a smooth user experience. By understanding the causes of runtime errors and employing effective debugging and error handling techniques, developers can build software that is more resilient, stable, and user-friendly.

Debugging techniques in the Delphi IDE are indispensable tools for identifying and resolving issues in software development. Delphi provides a comprehensive set of debugging features and tools that enable developers to efficiently track down and fix bugs in their applications. These techniques encompass various functionalities such as setting breakpoints, inspecting variables, evaluating expressions, stepping through code, and utilizing debugging windows. Leveraging these techniques, developers can effectively diagnose and rectify errors, ensuring the robustness and reliability of their Delphi applications.

One of the fundamental debugging techniques in Delphi is setting breakpoints, which allows developers to pause the execution of their program at specific points in the code. This enables them to examine the state of the program and identify the root cause of issues. To set a breakpoint in the Delphi IDE, developers simply click on the left margin of the code editor at the desired line or press F5. Alternatively, they can use the Toggle Breakpoint command from the context menu or toolbar.

Once breakpoints are set, developers can execute their program in debugging mode using the Run command or F9 key. When the program reaches a breakpoint during execution, it pauses, allowing developers to inspect the values of variables, evaluate expressions, and analyze the program's state. The Delphi IDE provides various debugging windows such as the Watches, Locals, Call Stack, and CPU windows, which display relevant information about the program's execution context, variables, and call stack.

In addition to breakpoints and debugging windows, Delphi offers powerful stepping techniques to navigate through code during debugging. Developers can step into (F7), step over (F8), or step out (Shift + F7) of functions and procedures, enabling them to trace the flow of execution and pinpoint errors. Stepping into a function or procedure allows developers to delve into its implementation and debug it line by line, while stepping over skips the execution of functions or procedures, focusing on the caller code instead. Stepping out exits the current function or procedure and returns to its caller.

Furthermore, Delphi provides advanced debugging features such as conditional breakpoints, which allow developers to break execution only when certain conditions are met. This enables targeted debugging and reduces the time spent analyzing irrelevant code paths. To create a conditional breakpoint in Delphi, developers right-click on the breakpoint marker, select Breakpoint Properties, and specify the desired conditions in the dialog box.

Another useful debugging technique in Delphi is the use of watches and expressions to monitor the values of variables and evaluate expressions during debugging. Developers can add watches to track specific variables or expressions and observe their values as the program executes. This helps in identifying unexpected changes in variables or evaluating complex expressions to debug intricate logic.

Moreover, Delphi offers integrated exception handling capabilities, allowing developers to catch and handle exceptions that occur during runtime. By using try-except blocks, developers can capture exceptions and gracefully handle them without causing the application to crash. Exception handling is vital for robust error management and ensuring the stability of Delphi applications under various conditions.

To deploy debugging techniques in the Delphi IDE, developers start by opening their project in the IDE and navigating to the source code containing the issue they want to debug. They then set breakpoints at relevant points in the code using the techniques described earlier. Once breakpoints are set, developers execute the program in debugging mode using the Run command or F9 key. As the program executes, developers use debugging windows, stepping techniques, watches, and expressions to analyze the program's behavior and identify bugs.

In summary, debugging techniques in the Delphi IDE are indispensable tools for software developers, enabling them to identify and resolve issues in their applications efficiently. By leveraging features such as breakpoints, debugging windows, stepping techniques, conditional breakpoints, watches, expressions, and exception handling, developers can debug their Delphi applications effectively and ensure their robustness and reliability. Mastering these debugging techniques is essential for delivering high-quality software and maintaining a smooth development workflow in Delphi.

Chapter 10: Best Practices for Efficient Code Editing in Delphi Pascal

Writing clean and maintainable code is a fundamental aspect of software development, ensuring that code is easy to understand, modify, and debug. Clean code follows established conventions, principles, and best practices, making it easier for developers to collaborate, maintain, and extend the codebase over time. To achieve clean and maintainable code, developers should adhere to coding standards, follow naming conventions, write modular and reusable code, use meaningful comments, and refactor code regularly. These tips help improve code readability, reduce complexity, and enhance the overall quality of the software.

One of the first tips for writing clean and maintainable code is to adhere to coding standards and guidelines. Coding standards define a set of rules and conventions for formatting code, naming variables, and organizing code structure. Following consistent coding standards across the codebase ensures that code is uniform and predictable, making it easier for developers to understand and navigate the code. In Delphi, developers can enforce coding standards using built-in tools such as the Delphi IDE's code formatting options and third-party code analysis tools.

Another essential tip is to follow naming conventions when naming variables, functions, classes, and other code elements. Meaningful and descriptive names provide valuable context and documentation for the code, making it easier to understand and maintain. In Delphi, developers typically use PascalCase for naming classes and types, camelCase for naming variables and parameters, and UPPERCASE for naming constants. By following consistent naming conventions, developers can improve code readability and convey the purpose of each code element effectively.

Writing modular and reusable code is also key to writing clean and maintainable code. Modular code breaks down complex tasks into smaller, self-contained modules or functions, each responsible for a specific aspect of the functionality. By modularizing code, developers can isolate functionality, promote code reuse, and facilitate testing and debugging. Delphi's support for object-oriented programming (OOP) encourages the creation of modular and reusable code through the use of classes, inheritance, and polymorphism.

Using meaningful comments and documentation is another important tip for writing clean and maintainable code. Comments provide additional context, explanations, and documentation for the code, helping other developers understand its purpose and functionality. Developers should use comments sparingly but effectively, focusing on explaining the why behind the code rather than stating the obvious. In addition to inline comments, developers can also use documentation tools such as Doxygen or PasDoc to generate documentation from comments in the source code.

Regular code refactoring is essential for maintaining clean and maintainable code over time. Refactoring involves restructuring and improving the internal structure of the code without changing its external behavior. By refactoring code regularly, developers can eliminate duplication, improve code clarity, and reduce complexity, leading to cleaner and more maintainable code. Delphi's refactoring tools and IDE features such as code navigation, code completion, and code analysis can aid developers in identifying and performing refactorings effectively.

Adopting a test-driven development (TDD) approach can also contribute to writing clean and maintainable code. TDD involves writing automated tests for code before implementing the actual functionality, ensuring that the code is testable, modular, and loosely coupled. By writing tests first, developers can clarify requirements, validate assumptions, and design cleaner and more maintainable code upfront. Delphi supports unit testing through frameworks such as DUnit or DelphiMocks, allowing developers to write and execute tests directly within the IDE.

Furthermore, practicing version control and utilizing collaborative development tools can help maintain clean and maintainable code in a team environment.

Version control systems such as Git enable developers to track changes, collaborate on code, and revert to previous versions if necessary. By using branching, merging, and pull requests effectively, developers can ensure that changes are properly reviewed, tested, and integrated into the codebase without introducing regressions or breaking existing functionality.

To deploy the technique of writing clean and maintainable code in Delphi projects, developers should establish coding standards, naming conventions, and best practices upfront and adhere to them consistently throughout the development process. They should use the Delphi IDE's built-in tools and features to enforce coding standards, refactor code, write meaningful comments, and perform code analysis. Additionally, developers should integrate automated testing and continuous integration (CI) practices into their workflow to validate code changes and ensure code quality and stability.

In summary, writing clean and maintainable code is essential for creating software that is easy to understand, modify, and maintain over time. By following coding standards, naming conventions, writing modular and reusable code, using meaningful comments, refactoring regularly, adopting TDD practices, and utilizing version control and collaborative development tools, developers can improve code quality, productivity, and maintainability in Delphi projects. These tips help create a positive development experience, foster collaboration, and ensure the long-term success of software projects.

Enhancing productivity with IDE shortcuts and customizations is a vital aspect of optimizing the development workflow and streamlining the coding process. IDEs (Integrated Development Environments) like Delphi offer a plethora of built-in shortcuts, features, and customization options that developers can leverage to boost efficiency, minimize repetitive tasks, and accelerate development. By mastering keyboard shortcuts, configuring personalized settings, and creating custom macros or scripts, developers can tailor their IDE environment to suit their preferences and maximize productivity.

One of the most straightforward ways to enhance productivity in the Delphi IDE is by mastering built-in keyboard shortcuts. These shortcuts enable developers to perform common tasks quickly and efficiently without relying on mouse clicks or navigating through menus. For example, in Delphi, pressing Ctrl + Shift + C automatically comments out the selected code, while Ctrl + Shift + U uncomments it. Similarly, Ctrl + Shift + Up/Down Arrow moves lines of code up or down, facilitating code reordering and restructuring.

Another productivity-enhancing technique is to customize the IDE layout and appearance to better suit individual preferences and workflow. Delphi allows users to rearrange tool windows, dock or undock panels, resize windows, and adjust font sizes and colors according to personal preferences. By organizing tool windows and panels in a way that optimizes workflow and reduces clutter, developers can create a more ergonomic and efficient working environment.

Additionally, Delphi supports the creation of custom keyboard shortcuts and macros, enabling developers to automate repetitive tasks or sequences of actions. By defining custom key bindings for frequently used commands or macros, developers can execute complex operations with a single keystroke, saving time and effort. Delphi's built-in macro recorder allows developers to record a series of actions and replay them later, automating repetitive tasks such as code refactoring or debugging.

Furthermore, Delphi's code templates and snippet library provide a convenient way to insert commonly used code snippets or boilerplate code into the editor with minimal effort. By creating and customizing code templates for frequently used code patterns or constructs, developers can reduce typing and ensure consistency across their codebase. Delphi's code insight feature also offers intelligent code completion suggestions and context-aware hints, further speeding up the coding process and reducing errors.

In addition to keyboard shortcuts and macros, Delphi allows developers to extend the IDE's functionality through plugins and third-party tools. Plugins such as

GExperts or Castalia offer additional features, refactorings, and productivity tools that complement the built-in capabilities of the Delphi IDE. By installing and configuring plugins that align with their specific needs and workflow, developers can further enhance productivity and streamline development tasks.

Deploying these productivity-enhancing techniques in the Delphi IDE involves familiarizing oneself with the available keyboard shortcuts, customization options, and plugin ecosystem. Developers can explore the IDE settings and preferences to customize the layout, appearance, and behavior of the IDE to their liking. They can also experiment with creating custom keyboard shortcuts, macros, and code templates to automate repetitive tasks and streamline their workflow.

Furthermore, developers can leverage online resources, forums, and community discussions to discover new productivity tips and tricks, share best practices, and learn from experienced Delphi developers. Participating in online communities and forums such as Stack Overflow, Delphi Forums, or the Embarcadero Community allows developers to exchange ideas, seek assistance, and stay updated on the latest developments in Delphi programming.

In summary, enhancing productivity with IDE shortcuts and customizations is essential for optimizing the development workflow and maximizing efficiency in Delphi programming. By mastering keyboard shortcuts, customizing IDE settings, creating custom macros and code templates, and leveraging plugins and third-party tools, developers can streamline their workflow, reduce repetitive tasks, and focus on writing high-quality code. Investing time in learning and mastering these productivity-enhancing techniques can significantly improve productivity and effectiveness in Delphi development projects.

BOOK 2
FROM BASICS TO BRILLIANCE
VISUAL DESIGNING IN DELPHI PASCAL PROGRAMMING

ROB BOTWRIGHT

Chapter 1: Introduction to Visual Designing in Delphi Pascal

Principles of visual design form the foundation of creating aesthetically pleasing and effective graphical user interfaces (GUIs) and user experiences (UX). Visual design principles encompass fundamental concepts and guidelines that govern the arrangement, composition, and presentation of visual elements in design. By understanding and applying these principles, designers can create visually appealing, intuitive, and engaging interfaces that effectively communicate information and facilitate user interaction.

One of the fundamental principles of visual design is balance, which refers to the distribution of visual elements within a design to create a sense of equilibrium and harmony. Balance can be achieved through symmetrical, asymmetrical, or radial arrangements of elements, depending on the desired visual effect. Symmetrical balance involves mirroring elements on either side of a central axis, creating a sense of stability and formality. Asymmetrical balance, on the other hand, involves distributing elements unevenly across the composition while maintaining visual equilibrium through contrast and hierarchy. Radial balance organizes elements around a central point, radiating outward in a circular or spiral pattern.

Another important principle is contrast, which involves creating visual distinction and emphasis by juxtaposing elements with different characteristics such as color, size, shape, or texture. Contrast helps draw attention to important elements, establish hierarchy, and create visual interest. For example, contrasting colors or sizes can highlight key elements such as buttons, headings, or call-to-action items, making them stand out from surrounding content.

Unity, or cohesion, is another key principle that focuses on creating a sense of cohesion and coherence throughout a design. Unity involves establishing visual consistency and harmony by using consistent styles, colors, typography, and imagery across different parts of the interface. Consistent use of design elements helps reinforce the brand identity, establish visual continuity, and create a seamless user experience.

Hierarchy is another crucial principle that guides the organization and prioritization of visual elements within a design. Hierarchy involves arranging elements in a structured manner to convey importance, sequence, or relationship. By establishing a clear hierarchy of elements through visual cues such as size, color, contrast, or placement, designers can guide users' attention, facilitate navigation, and improve comprehension. For example, larger headings or bolder colors can indicate primary content or actions, while smaller text or muted colors can denote secondary or supporting information.

Proportion and scale are also important principles that govern the relative size and proportion of elements within a design. Proportion involves ensuring that elements are appropriately sized and scaled relative to each other and the overall composition. Maintaining proper proportion and scale helps create visual balance, hierarchy, and readability. For example, oversized elements can overwhelm the design and distract users, while undersized elements may go unnoticed or appear insignificant.

Another key principle is emphasis, which involves highlighting important elements or focal points within a design to attract users' attention and convey meaning. Emphasis can be achieved through various visual techniques such as contrast, color, size, position, or animation. By strategically emphasizing key elements such as headlines, buttons, or images, designers can guide users' focus and enhance the effectiveness of the design.

Additionally, white space, or negative space, plays a crucial role in visual design by providing breathing room and balance within a composition. White space refers to the empty or unused space between and around elements in a design. By incorporating adequate white space, designers can improve readability, create visual separation, and reduce clutter, enhancing the overall aesthetics and usability of the interface.

To deploy these principles of visual design effectively in digital projects, designers can use design software such as Adobe Photoshop, Illustrator, or Sketch to create mockups, wireframes, and prototypes. These tools provide a range of features and functionalities for arranging, styling, and manipulating visual elements to achieve desired design outcomes. Once the design is finalized, designers can collaborate with developers to implement the design using front-end technologies such as HTML, CSS, and JavaScript.

In summary, principles of visual design are essential guidelines that inform the creation of visually appealing and effective user interfaces and experiences. By understanding and applying these principles such as balance, contrast, unity, hierarchy, proportion, emphasis, and white space, designers can create designs that are not only aesthetically pleasing but also functional, intuitive, and user-friendly. Mastery of visual design principles empowers designers to craft compelling and engaging digital experiences that resonate with users and achieve business objectives.

The importance of visual design in software development cannot be overstated, as it plays a crucial role in shaping user perceptions, enhancing usability, and driving user engagement. Visual design encompasses the aesthetic aspects of software interfaces, including layout, typography, color, imagery, and overall visual presentation. Effective visual design not only makes software visually appealing but also contributes to improved user experience, increased user satisfaction, and ultimately, the success of the software product.

Visual design is critical in software development because it is often the first impression users have of a product. The visual design of an application or website is the initial point of contact for users, influencing their perception of the brand, professionalism, and quality of the software. A visually appealing interface can capture users' attention, instill confidence, and create a positive impression, encouraging users to explore further and engage with the software.

Moreover, visual design plays a significant role in establishing the usability and intuitiveness of software interfaces. Well-designed interfaces are intuitive, easy to navigate, and visually coherent, allowing users to interact with the software effortlessly and accomplish their tasks efficiently. By employing principles of visual hierarchy, consistency, and clarity, designers can guide users' attention, communicate information effectively, and streamline the user experience. For example, clear labeling, intuitive iconography, and logical layout contribute to improved navigation and usability, reducing user frustration and increasing productivity.

In addition to usability, visual design also influences user engagement and retention. Visually engaging interfaces captivate users' attention and encourage exploration, leading to increased user engagement and longer retention periods. Design elements such as vibrant colors, appealing graphics, and interactive animations can enhance user experience, evoke emotional responses, and foster a connection between users and the software. By creating visually engaging experiences, software developers can create memorable interactions that leave a lasting impression on users and encourage repeat usage.

Furthermore, visual design plays a crucial role in brand identity and differentiation in the competitive software market. Consistent visual branding across software interfaces helps reinforce brand identity, establish brand recognition, and foster brand loyalty. A cohesive visual identity communicates brand values, personality, and positioning, distinguishing the software product from competitors and enhancing its perceived value in the eyes of users. Through strategic use of color, typography, imagery, and other design elements, software developers can create cohesive brand experiences that resonate with users and strengthen brand equity.

Moreover, visual design is essential for conveying information and guiding user behavior within software interfaces. Effective use of visual hierarchy, typography, and imagery can help users understand complex information, prioritize tasks, and make informed decisions. By presenting information in a clear, concise, and visually appealing manner, designers can facilitate comprehension and decision-making, leading to improved user satisfaction and task success rates. For example, data visualization techniques such as charts, graphs, and infographics can help users interpret data more effectively and derive insights from complex datasets.

Additionally, visual design plays a crucial role in accessibility and inclusivity in software development. Accessible design ensures that software interfaces are usable and navigable by users of all abilities, including those with disabilities or impairments. Design considerations such as color contrast, font size, keyboard navigation, and screen reader compatibility are essential for creating inclusive user experiences that accommodate diverse user needs and preferences. By prioritizing accessibility in visual design, software developers can ensure that their products are accessible to everyone, regardless of physical or cognitive limitations.

To deploy effective visual design in software development projects, designers and developers must collaborate closely to integrate design considerations into the development process. Designers use tools such as Adobe XD, Sketch, or Figma to create wireframes, mockups, and prototypes that visualize the intended visual design of the software interface. Once the design is finalized, developers implement the design using front-end technologies such as HTML, CSS, and JavaScript, ensuring that the visual design is faithfully translated into code. Continuous feedback and iteration between designers and developers are essential to refine the visual design and address any implementation challenges or constraints.

In summary, visual design is a critical aspect of software development that influences user perceptions, usability, engagement, and brand identity. Effective visual design creates visually appealing, intuitive, and engaging software interfaces that enhance user experience, drive user engagement, and differentiate the software product in the competitive market. By prioritizing visual design principles and integrating design considerations into the development process, software developers can create compelling and memorable user experiences that resonate with users and contribute to the success of their software products.

Chapter 2: Exploring the Delphi Form Designer

Navigating the Form Designer interface is an essential skill for developers working with graphical user interface (GUI) applications in development environments like Delphi. The Form Designer is a visual design tool that allows developers to create, design, and layout user interface components for their applications. Understanding how to effectively navigate the Form Designer interface enables developers to efficiently design and customize user interfaces, streamline development workflows, and create visually appealing and functional applications.

In Delphi, accessing the Form Designer interface is straightforward. Developers typically open the IDE (Integrated Development Environment) and create a new project or open an existing one. Once inside the IDE, they can navigate to the Form Designer by selecting the form file associated with the application they are working on. This can be done by either double-clicking on the form file in the Project Manager window or selecting it from the Project Explorer. Alternatively, developers can use the "File" menu and choose "Open" to locate and open the form file directly.

Once inside the Form Designer interface, developers are presented with a visual representation of the form or window that represents the application's user interface. The Form Designer provides a canvas where developers can drag and drop visual components such as buttons, labels, text boxes, and other UI controls onto the form. These components can then be resized, positioned, and customized using the properties editor and context menus.

Navigating the Form Designer interface involves familiarizing oneself with the various tools, controls, and features available for designing and customizing user interfaces. The Form Designer typically includes a toolbox or palette that contains a wide range of UI components that developers can use to build their application's interface. These components are categorized and organized for easy access, allowing developers to quickly find and add the desired controls to their form.

In Delphi's Form Designer, developers can navigate the toolbox using the mouse or keyboard shortcuts. They can scroll through the list of available components, collapse or expand categories, and search for specific components using the search bar. Once they have located the desired component, they can simply drag it from the toolbox onto the form canvas to add it to their application's interface.

Once components are added to the form, developers can further customize and configure them using the properties editor. The properties editor allows developers to view and modify various properties and settings of the selected component, such as its size, position, appearance, behavior, and event handlers. Developers can navigate through the list of properties using the keyboard or mouse and make changes directly within the properties editor.

In addition to adding and customizing UI components, developers can also navigate and manage the layout of their form using alignment and spacing tools. The Form Designer typically includes options for aligning components relative to each other, distributing components evenly, and resizing components to fit the form's dimensions. These layout tools help developers create visually appealing and well-organized user interfaces that adapt to different screen sizes and resolutions.

Another essential aspect of navigating the Form Designer interface is understanding how to work with multiple forms or windows within a single application. In Delphi, developers can easily switch between different forms using tabs or tabs in the IDE's editor area. They can also use the "View" menu to navigate to specific forms or switch between open forms quickly. This allows developers to work on different parts of their application's user interface simultaneously and maintain a cohesive design across all forms.

Furthermore, navigating the Form Designer interface involves understanding how to preview and test the application's interface during the design process. In Delphi, developers can switch between design view and code view to see how their changes affect the appearance and behavior of the application. They can also use the "Run" or "Debug" commands to compile and execute the application, allowing them to interact with the user interface and test its functionality in real-time.

To deploy these techniques effectively, developers should practice regularly using the Form Designer interface and familiarize themselves with its various features and capabilities. They can experiment with different UI components, layouts, and customization options to gain proficiency and confidence in designing user interfaces. Additionally, developers can explore online tutorials, documentation, and community forums for tips, tricks, and best practices for navigating the Form Designer interface and designing compelling user interfaces in Delphi applications.

In summary, navigating the Form Designer interface is a fundamental skill for developers working with GUI applications in Delphi. By mastering the tools, controls, and features available in the Form Designer, developers can efficiently design, customize, and test user interfaces for their applications. With practice and experimentation, developers can create visually appealing, intuitive, and functional user interfaces that enhance the overall user experience and contribute to the success of their software projects.

Understanding layout and alignment tools is crucial for creating visually appealing and well-organized user interfaces in software development. These tools provide developers with the means to precisely position and arrange UI components on a form or window, ensuring consistency, readability, and usability across different screen sizes and resolutions. By mastering layout and alignment tools, developers can create responsive and flexible user interfaces that adapt to various devices and display settings, enhancing the overall user experience and usability of their applications.

In graphical user interface (GUI) design, layout refers to the arrangement of UI components such as buttons, labels, text fields, and images within a form or window. Effective layout design ensures that UI components are organized logically and aesthetically, making it easy for users to navigate and interact with the application. Layout tools provide developers with the ability to manipulate the size, position, and spacing of UI components to achieve the desired visual hierarchy and structure.

One of the primary layout tools available in GUI design is the grid system. Grid-based layouts divide the form or window into a series of rows and columns, allowing developers to align UI components along horizontal and vertical axes. Grid systems provide a consistent and predictable structure for organizing UI elements, making it easier to maintain alignment and spacing across the interface. Developers can adjust the size and spacing of grid cells to accommodate different content and screen sizes, ensuring a consistent layout across devices.

Another common layout tool is the anchoring mechanism, which allows developers to specify how UI components should behave when the form or window is resized. Anchoring controls anchor UI components to the edges or corners of the form or to other adjacent components, ensuring that they maintain their position and size relative to the form's dimensions. By anchoring components strategically, developers can create responsive layouts that adapt to changes in screen size and orientation, providing a seamless user experience on different devices.

Alignment tools are essential for ensuring that UI components are positioned consistently and precisely within the layout. Alignment tools allow developers to align UI components along horizontal and vertical axes, ensuring that they are evenly spaced and visually balanced. Common alignment options include left alignment, right alignment, center alignment, top alignment, bottom alignment, and middle alignment. By aligning components with each other or with the edges of the form, developers can create a cohesive and visually appealing layout that guides users' attention and enhances readability.

In addition to alignment, spacing tools are essential for controlling the distance between UI components and maintaining visual balance within the layout. Spacing tools allow developers to adjust the margins and padding around UI components, ensuring that there is sufficient space between components to prevent overcrowding and improve readability. Developers can specify the spacing between components horizontally and vertically, as well as adjust the spacing between groups of components or between components and the edges of the form.

Understanding how to use layout and alignment tools effectively involves mastering the features and functionalities of the GUI design software or development environment being used. In IDEs like Delphi, developers can access layout and alignment tools through the Form Designer interface, which provides a visual representation of the form or window and allows developers to manipulate UI components using drag-and-drop gestures, mouse clicks, and keyboard shortcuts.

In Delphi's Form Designer, developers can access layout and alignment tools through the properties editor and context menus. The properties editor allows developers to specify the size, position, anchoring, and alignment properties of UI components, while the context menus provide quick access to common layout and alignment commands such as aligning components to the left, right, top, or bottom edges of the form.

To deploy layout and alignment techniques effectively in Delphi applications, developers should experiment with different layout options and alignment settings to find the optimal configuration for their user interface. They can use the Form Designer interface to visually preview and adjust the layout of their forms, making incremental changes as needed to achieve the desired visual hierarchy and structure. Additionally, developers can test their layouts on different devices and screen resolutions to ensure that they remain responsive and adaptable to varying display settings.

In summary, understanding layout and alignment tools is essential for creating visually appealing, organized, and responsive user interfaces in software development. By mastering grid systems, anchoring mechanisms, alignment options, and spacing tools, developers can create layouts that are visually balanced, consistent, and user-friendly. With practice and experimentation, developers can leverage layout and alignment tools to create compelling and intuitive user interfaces that enhance the overall user experience and usability of their applications.

Chapter 3: Understanding Components and Controls

An overview of built-in components and controls is essential for developers embarking on software development projects, as these elements form the foundation of user interface design and functionality. Built-in components and controls are pre-defined visual elements that developers can incorporate into their applications to enable user interaction, display information, and enhance usability. By understanding the capabilities and characteristics of these components, developers can leverage them effectively to create intuitive, visually appealing, and feature-rich applications that meet user requirements and expectations.

In software development, built-in components and controls encompass a wide range of UI elements that serve various purposes and functions. These components include buttons, labels, text boxes, check boxes, radio buttons, list boxes, combo boxes, progress bars, sliders, scroll bars, menus, toolbars, tabs, trees, grids, and many more. Each component is designed to perform specific tasks or provide specific functionality within the application's user interface, allowing users to interact with the software and perform actions such as inputting data, making selections, navigating menus, and viewing information.

Buttons are one of the most common and versatile built-in components, used to trigger actions or commands within the application. Buttons can be customized with text, icons, and images, and can respond to user interactions such as clicks or taps. Developers can use buttons to implement features such as submitting forms, saving data, navigating between screens, or executing commands.

Labels are another essential built-in component used for displaying text or descriptive information within the user interface. Labels are often used to provide context or instructions to users, explain the purpose of other UI elements, or display dynamic information such as status messages or error notifications. Developers can customize labels with different fonts, colors, and styles to enhance readability and visual appeal.

Text boxes and input fields allow users to input text or numeric data into the application. Text boxes can be single-line or multi-line, depending on the amount of data users are expected to input. Developers can set properties such as maximum length, input format, and validation rules to control the behavior and appearance of text boxes and ensure data integrity.

Check boxes and radio buttons are used for allowing users to make selections or choose options from a list of predefined choices. Check boxes allow users to select multiple options simultaneously, while radio buttons restrict users to selecting only one option from a group of choices. These components are commonly used in forms, settings screens, and preference dialogs to enable users to customize their experience and make selections.

List boxes, combo boxes, and drop-down menus are used for presenting a list of options or choices to users in a compact and organized format. List boxes display a list of items that users can select from, while combo boxes combine a text box with a drop-down list of options, allowing users to either select an option from the list or input a custom value. Drop-down menus provide hierarchical navigation and categorization of options, allowing users to access commands or features grouped under different categories or menus.

Progress bars, sliders, and scroll bars are used for visualizing and controlling the progress or position of a process or operation within the application. Progress bars indicate the completion status of a task or operation, providing users with feedback on the progress and duration of ongoing processes. Sliders allow users to adjust values or settings within a predefined range by dragging a handle along a track, while scroll bars enable users to navigate through content that exceeds the visible area of a window or container.

Menus, toolbars, and tabs are used for organizing and accessing commands, features, and functionality within the application. Menus provide a hierarchical structure for grouping commands and options under different categories or submenus, allowing users to access commands through a series of nested menus. Toolbars contain a set of icons or buttons representing commonly used commands or actions, providing users with quick access to frequently performed tasks. Tabs organize content into separate sections or pages within the application, allowing users to switch between different views or modes.

Trees and grids are used for displaying hierarchical or tabular data in a structured and organized manner. Trees present data in a hierarchical format with expandable and collapsible nodes, allowing users to navigate through levels of information and drill down into details. Grids display data in rows and columns, providing users with a structured view of tabular data that can be sorted, filtered, and manipulated.

To deploy built-in components and controls in software development projects, developers can use integrated development environments (IDEs) such as Delphi, Visual Studio, or Xcode, which provide a visual design environment for designing and customizing user interfaces. In Delphi, developers can access built-in components and controls through the Form Designer interface, where they can drag and drop components onto the form canvas and configure their properties using the Object Inspector.

Once the components are added to the form, developers can write event handlers and logic to define the behavior and functionality of the components. For example, developers can write code to handle button clicks, validate input in text boxes, respond to selection changes in list boxes, or update the state of progress bars dynamically. By combining built-in components with custom code, developers can create interactive and dynamic user interfaces that meet the specific requirements of their applications.

In summary, understanding the capabilities and characteristics of built-in components and controls is essential for developers to create intuitive, visually appealing, and feature-rich user interfaces in software development projects. By leveraging built-in components effectively and combining them with custom code, developers can create applications that provide a seamless and engaging user experience, driving user satisfaction and adoption. With practice and experimentation, developers can harness the power of built-in components to design and develop innovative and compelling software applications that meet the needs and expectations of modern users.

Customizing components for specific tasks is a fundamental aspect of software development, allowing developers to tailor the behavior, appearance, and functionality of built-in components to meet the unique requirements of their applications. By customizing components, developers can extend their capabilities, enhance user experience, and achieve greater flexibility and control over the application's behavior. Understanding how to customize components effectively enables developers to create highly specialized and optimized solutions that address specific use cases and deliver maximum value to users.

In software development, customizing components involves modifying their properties, styles, event handlers, and behavior to align with the desired functionality and user experience. This customization process can vary depending on the requirements of the application and the capabilities of the development environment or framework being used. Developers can leverage various techniques and tools to customize components effectively, ranging from simple property adjustments to more advanced programming and design strategies.

One common technique for customizing components is modifying their properties and settings to control their appearance and behavior. In integrated development environments (IDEs) like Delphi, developers can access the properties of components through the Object Inspector, where they can adjust settings such as size, color, font, alignment, visibility, and enabled state. By tweaking these properties, developers can achieve the desired visual style and behavior for the components, ensuring consistency and coherence within the user interface.

For example, developers can customize the appearance of buttons by changing their colors, fonts, and sizes to match the application's branding or visual theme. They can also modify the text displayed on the buttons to provide clear and meaningful labels that guide users' interactions. Similarly, developers can adjust the properties of text boxes and input fields to specify input formats, validation rules, and default values, ensuring data integrity and user input accuracy.

Another technique for customizing components is implementing custom event handlers to define their behavior in response to user interactions or system events. Event handlers are functions or methods that are executed when specific events occur, such as button clicks, mouse movements, key presses, or data changes. By writing custom event handlers, developers can add interactivity and functionality to components, enabling them to respond dynamically to user actions and external stimuli.

In Delphi, developers can define event handlers for components by double-clicking on them in the Form Designer interface, which automatically generates stub procedures for handling common events such as OnClick, OnChange, or OnKeyDown. Developers can then write custom code within these event handlers to perform tasks such as validating input, updating data, triggering actions, or navigating to other parts of the application. By implementing custom event handlers, developers can extend the capabilities of components and create interactive user interfaces that engage and empower users.

Additionally, developers can leverage inheritance and subclassing techniques to create custom components that extend or enhance the functionality of existing built-in components. In object-oriented programming (OOP) languages like Delphi, developers can derive new classes from existing component classes and override or extend their methods and properties to add custom behavior or features. This approach allows developers to encapsulate complex functionality within reusable and modular components, promoting code reusability and maintainability.

For example, developers can create a custom button component that includes additional features such as hover effects, animated transitions, or context-sensitive tooltips. By subclassing the standard button component and adding custom code to handle mouse events and drawing routines, developers can enhance the visual appeal and interactivity of the button while maintaining compatibility with existing code and design patterns.

Moreover, developers can utilize third-party libraries, frameworks, or component packages to access a wider range of pre-built components and customization options. Many software development platforms offer extensive libraries of third-party components and controls that provide advanced functionality and features beyond what is available in the standard library. By integrating these components into their applications, developers can leverage the expertise and innovation of the wider developer community and accelerate the development process.

In Delphi, developers can install and use third-party component packages by adding them to the IDE's component palette and dragging them onto the form canvas like built-in components. These third-party components often come with their own set of properties, methods, and event handlers that developers can customize to suit their specific requirements. By incorporating third-party components into their applications, developers can access specialized functionality such as data visualization, charting, reporting, or advanced user interface controls that would be time-consuming or challenging to implement from scratch.

To deploy these customization techniques effectively, developers should have a thorough understanding of the capabilities and limitations of the components they are working with, as well as the programming languages, frameworks, and development tools they are using. They should also consider factors such as performance, usability, accessibility, and compatibility when customizing components to ensure that the resulting applications meet the needs and expectations of their users.

In summary, customizing components for specific tasks is a critical aspect of software development that enables developers to create tailored solutions that address the unique requirements of their applications. By leveraging techniques such as modifying properties, implementing custom event handlers, subclassing components, and integrating third-party libraries, developers can extend the capabilities of built-in components and create highly specialized and optimized user interfaces. With creativity, skill, and attention to detail, developers can craft compelling and effective applications that deliver value and enhance the user experience.

Chapter 4: Working with Properties and Events

Manipulating properties of components is a fundamental aspect of software development, enabling developers to customize the appearance, behavior, and functionality of user interface elements within their applications. Properties represent the characteristics or attributes of components, such as their size, color, font, visibility, and enabled state, and can be modified dynamically to achieve desired effects and behaviors. By understanding how to manipulate properties effectively, developers can create visually appealing, interactive, and user-friendly applications that meet the specific requirements and preferences of their users.

In software development, properties serve as the building blocks of user interfaces, providing developers with fine-grained control over the appearance and behavior of components. Each component exposes a set of properties that can be accessed and modified programmatically to achieve the desired presentation and functionality. For example, in Delphi, developers can access and modify properties of components using the Object Inspector in the integrated development environment (IDE), which provides a visual interface for inspecting and editing the properties of selected components.

To manipulate properties of components in Delphi, developers can select the desired component on the form canvas or in the component hierarchy and then use the Object Inspector to view and modify its properties. The Object Inspector displays a list of properties organized into categories, allowing developers to navigate and modify them conveniently. Developers can modify properties by typing values directly into the corresponding fields in the Object Inspector or by selecting options from drop-down lists or color pickers.

For example, developers can change the background color of a button component by selecting the Button component on the form canvas, locating the Color property in the Object Inspector, and then choosing a new color from the color picker. Similarly, developers can adjust the font size of a label component by selecting the Label component, locating the Font property, and then specifying the desired font size in points.

In addition to modifying properties through the Object Inspector, developers can manipulate properties programmatically using code. This allows developers to change properties dynamically at runtime based on user input, system events, or other programmatic conditions. In Delphi, properties of components can be accessed and modified using the dot notation, where the component name is followed by a period (.) and the property name.

For example, developers can change the text displayed on a label component programmatically by assigning a new value to its Caption property. Similarly, developers can change the visibility of a button component by setting its Visible property to True or False. By manipulating properties programmatically, developers can create dynamic and responsive user interfaces that adapt to changing conditions and user interactions.

Furthermore, developers can use conditional statements, loops, and other control structures to apply property changes selectively based on specific criteria or conditions. This allows developers to implement complex logic for modifying properties dynamically in response to user actions or system events. For example, developers can use an if statement to change the background color of a button component when it is clicked or use a loop to iterate over a collection of components and apply property changes to each one.

To deploy property manipulation techniques effectively, developers should have a clear understanding of the properties available for each component and their respective meanings and effects. They should also consider factors such as usability, accessibility, and performance when modifying properties to ensure that the resulting user interface is intuitive, inclusive, and efficient. Additionally, developers should test their applications thoroughly to verify that property changes behave as expected and do not introduce unintended side effects or errors.

In summary, manipulating properties of components is a powerful technique in software development that allows developers to customize the appearance, behavior, and functionality of user interface elements within their applications. By understanding how to access and modify properties using visual tools and code, developers can create rich, interactive, and user-friendly applications that meet the needs and expectations of their users. With careful consideration and experimentation, developers can leverage property manipulation techniques to create compelling and effective user interfaces that enhance the overall user experience.

Handling events to create interactive interfaces is a fundamental aspect of software development, empowering developers to respond to user actions, system events, and other stimuli in real-time. Events represent occurrences or changes within an application, such as button clicks, mouse movements, key presses, or data updates, and can trigger predefined actions or behaviors. By understanding how to handle events effectively, developers can create dynamic, responsive, and engaging user interfaces that provide intuitive and seamless user experiences.

In software development, events are an integral part of the user interface (UI) design and programming paradigm, enabling developers to create interactive and responsive applications that engage users and facilitate effective communication. Each user action or system event generates one or more events, which are dispatched to event handlers or callback functions responsible for processing and responding to them. Event handling involves associating event handlers with specific UI components or system objects and defining the logic or behavior to execute when the corresponding events occur.

To handle events effectively, developers must first identify the events they want to respond to and then define appropriate event handlers to process them. In integrated development environments (IDEs) like Delphi, developers can access event handlers for UI components through the Object Inspector or code editor, where they can define callback functions or methods to handle specific events. For example, developers can define an OnClick event handler for a button component to execute a specific action when the button is clicked by the user.

In Delphi, handling events involves defining event handlers for components by assigning callback functions or methods to specific event properties. For example, to handle the OnClick event of a button component, developers can write a procedure or method that performs the desired action and then assign it to the button's OnClick event property using the Object Inspector or code editor. This associates the event handler with the button component and ensures that the specified action is executed when the button is clicked.

delphiCopy code

```
procedure    TForm1.Button1Click(Sender:    TObject);
begin // Perform action when button is clicked end;
```

In addition to handling events for UI components, developers can also handle system-level events, such as timer events, keyboard events, mouse events, or form events, to create more interactive and responsive interfaces. For example, developers can use timer events to trigger periodic updates or animations within the application, keyboard events to capture user input from the keyboard, mouse events to track user interactions with graphical elements, or form events to monitor changes in the application's state or lifecycle.

To handle system-level events in Delphi, developers can use predefined event handlers provided by the VCL (Visual Component Library) framework or define custom event handlers to respond to specific events. For example, to handle timer events, developers can create a TTimer component, set its interval and enabled properties, and then define an OnTimer event handler to execute the desired action when the timer expires.

delphiCopy code

```
procedure    TForm1.Timer1Timer(Sender:    TObject);
begin // Perform action when timer expires end;
```

Furthermore, developers can leverage event propagation and bubbling mechanisms to handle events at different levels of the application hierarchy and delegate event handling to parent or container components. Event propagation allows events to be dispatched from child components to parent components, enabling centralized event handling and coordination across multiple components. By capturing events at higher levels of the hierarchy, developers can implement common event handling logic or manage interactions between nested components more efficiently.

To deploy event handling techniques effectively, developers should have a clear understanding of the events available for each component or system object and their respective triggers and behaviors. They should also consider factors such as event sequencing, event priorities, and event propagation rules when designing event-driven applications to ensure consistent and predictable behavior. Additionally, developers should test their event handling logic thoroughly to verify that events are handled correctly and that the application responds appropriately to user interactions and system events.

In summary, handling events to create interactive interfaces is a critical aspect of software development that enables developers to create dynamic, responsive, and engaging user experiences. By understanding how to identify, define, and handle events effectively, developers can create applications that respond intuitively to user actions and provide seamless interactions. With careful planning and implementation, developers can leverage event handling techniques to create compelling and effective user interfaces that meet the needs and expectations of their users.

Chapter 5: Layout Management and Alignment Techniques

Strategies for effective layout design are essential for creating user interfaces that are visually appealing, intuitive to navigate, and optimized for usability across different devices and screen sizes. Layout design encompasses the arrangement and organization of UI components, such as buttons, text fields, images, and menus, within a window, form, or webpage, to create a coherent and cohesive user experience. By employing proven strategies and best practices, developers can create layouts that enhance usability, readability, and accessibility while conveying information effectively and guiding users through tasks and workflows.

One fundamental strategy for effective layout design is to prioritize simplicity and clarity in the arrangement of UI components. A cluttered or overly complex layout can overwhelm users and hinder their ability to focus on essential tasks or information. To achieve simplicity, developers should aim to minimize visual noise and unnecessary elements, prioritize the placement of key components and content, and maintain consistent spacing, alignment, and hierarchy throughout the layout.

In web development, developers can use CSS (Cascading Style Sheets) frameworks like Bootstrap or Flexbox to create responsive and grid-based layouts that adapt to different screen sizes and orientations. By defining grid systems and responsive breakpoints, developers can ensure that UI components are arranged logically and proportionally across various devices, from desktop computers to smartphones and tablets. For example, developers can use the Bootstrap grid system to divide the layout into rows and columns and then place UI components within grid cells using predefined CSS classes.

cssCopy code

```css
<div class="container"> <div class="row"> <div class="col-md-6">Left Column</div> <div class="col-md-6">Right Column</div> </div> </div>
```

Another strategy for effective layout design is to consider the natural flow of information and user interactions within the application. By organizing UI components in a logical sequence that mirrors the user's mental model and expected workflow, developers can enhance usability and streamline navigation. For example, in a form-based application, developers can arrange input fields and buttons in the order in which users are likely to encounter them, starting with essential information and progressing through optional or supplementary fields.

Moreover, developers can use visual hierarchy and emphasis techniques to draw attention to important elements and guide users' focus within the layout. By employing techniques such as contrasting colors, varying font sizes and weights, and strategic placement of visual elements like icons and call-to-action buttons, developers can create layouts that prioritize critical information and encourage desired user interactions.

For example, developers can use larger and bolder fonts for headings and titles to make them stand out from body text, or they can use color accents to highlight interactive elements like buttons or links.

In addition to visual hierarchy, developers can use whitespace effectively to improve readability and reduce cognitive load within the layout. Whitespace, or negative space, refers to the empty or unused areas between UI components and content elements. By strategically incorporating whitespace around text blocks, images, and interactive elements, developers can create breathing room and visual separation, making it easier for users to scan and digest information. Whitespace also helps prevent overcrowding and improves overall aesthetics by creating a sense of balance and harmony within the layout.

Furthermore, developers should consider the principles of responsive design when designing layouts for web applications or mobile apps. Responsive design aims to create interfaces that adapt fluidly to different screen sizes and orientations, providing a consistent and optimal experience across devices. To achieve responsive layouts, developers can use CSS media queries to apply specific styles based on the device's screen width or resolution. For example, developers can define breakpoints where the layout shifts from a multi-column desktop view to a single-column mobile view and adjust styles accordingly.

cssCopy code

```css
@media (max-width: 768px) { /* Apply styles for
mobile devices */ }
```

To deploy these layout design strategies effectively, developers should leverage prototyping and mockup tools to visualize and iterate on their designs before implementation. Tools like Adobe XD, Sketch, or Figma allow developers to create wireframes and interactive prototypes that simulate user interactions and screen transitions, enabling them to test and refine their layout designs iteratively. By soliciting feedback from users and stakeholders early in the design process, developers can identify potential usability issues or improvements and make necessary adjustments before finalizing the layout.

In summary, effective layout design is crucial for creating user interfaces that are visually appealing, intuitive to navigate, and optimized for usability across different devices and screen sizes. By prioritizing simplicity, clarity, and logical organization, developers can create layouts that enhance user experience and facilitate efficient interaction with the application. By employing visual hierarchy, whitespace, and responsive design techniques, developers can create layouts that prioritize essential information, improve readability, and adapt seamlessly to the diverse needs and preferences of users. With careful planning, iteration, and testing, developers can create layouts that elevate the overall user experience and contribute to the success of their applications.

Aligning components within containers is a crucial

aspect of user interface design, ensuring that UI elements are organized in a visually pleasing and logically structured manner. Proper alignment enhances readability, usability, and aesthetic appeal, contributing to a positive user experience. Developers can employ various alignment techniques to achieve desired layouts, including horizontal and vertical alignment, centering, distribution, and justification. By mastering these techniques, developers can create polished and professional-looking user interfaces that effectively communicate information and guide users through tasks.

Horizontal alignment is the positioning of components along the horizontal axis of a container, ensuring that they are evenly spaced and aligned relative to one another. In web development, developers can use CSS flexbox or grid layouts to achieve horizontal alignment effectively. Flexbox provides a flexible and powerful way to distribute space among components within a container, allowing developers to specify alignment properties such as justify-content and align-items to control the horizontal alignment of components.

cssCopy code

```
.container { display: flex; justify-content: space-between; /* Align items with space between */ }
```

Similarly, CSS grid layouts allow developers to define precise grid structures and specify alignment properties for rows and columns, enabling fine-grained control over the horizontal alignment of components. By setting the justify-items property to center or start, developers can align components horizontally within grid cells, ensuring consistency and coherence in the layout.

cssCopy code

.container { display: grid; grid-template-columns: repeat(3, 1fr); /* Three equal-width columns */ justify-items: center; /* Align items horizontally at the center */ }

Vertical alignment, on the other hand, refers to the positioning of components along the vertical axis of a container, ensuring that they are aligned relative to one another vertically. In web development, developers can use CSS properties such as align-items and align-self to control vertical alignment within flexbox containers. By setting the align-items property to center or stretch, developers can align components vertically within the container, ensuring consistent vertical spacing and alignment.

cssCopy code

.container { display: flex; align-items: center; /* Align items vertically at the center */ }

In addition to horizontal and vertical alignment, developers can use centering techniques to position components at the center of a container both horizontally and vertically. In CSS, centering components can be achieved using a combination of flexbox or grid layouts and margin properties. For example, to center a component horizontally within a container, developers can set the margin property to auto on both sides of the component, effectively centering it within the container.

cssCopy code

```css
.component { margin-left: auto; margin-right: auto; }
```

To center a component vertically within a container, developers can use flexbox or grid layouts to align items vertically at the center or use CSS properties such as position and transform to achieve vertical centering. By setting the position property to absolute and using the top and left properties to specify the position relative to the container, developers can center components vertically within the container.

cssCopy code

```css
.component { position: absolute; top: 50%; left: 50%;
transform: translate(-50%, -50%); }
```

Furthermore, developers can use distribution and justification techniques to evenly space components within a container or align them relative to container edges or boundaries. In CSS flexbox layouts, developers can use properties such as justify-content and align-content to control the distribution and alignment of components along the main and cross axes of the container. By setting the justify-content property to space-between or space-around, developers can evenly distribute space between or around components within the container, ensuring balanced and visually pleasing layouts.

cssCopy code

```css
.container { display: flex; justify-content: space-
between; /* Distribute items with space between */ }
```

Similarly, CSS grid layouts provide properties such as justify-items and align-items to control the justification and alignment of components within grid cells. By setting the justify-items property to center or start and the align-items property to center or stretch, developers can align components relative to the grid cell boundaries, ensuring consistent alignment and spacing within the layout.

cssCopy code

.container { display: grid; justify-items: center; /* Justify items horizontally at the center */ align-items: center; /* Align items vertically at the center */ }

To deploy these alignment techniques effectively, developers should consider factors such as content hierarchy, visual balance, and user expectations when designing layouts. They should also test their layouts across different devices and screen sizes to ensure consistent alignment and readability. By mastering alignment techniques and applying them judiciously, developers can create user interfaces that are visually appealing, easy to navigate, and optimized for usability and accessibility.

Chapter 6: Customizing User Interfaces with Graphics and Images

Integrating graphics and images into UI design is a pivotal aspect of creating visually engaging and immersive user experiences. Graphics and images serve multiple purposes within user interfaces, ranging from enhancing aesthetics and branding to conveying information and guiding user interactions. By strategically incorporating graphics and images, designers can captivate users' attention, communicate complex concepts more effectively, and evoke desired emotions or responses. Moreover, advancements in technology and design tools have expanded the possibilities for integrating graphics and images into UI design, allowing designers to create rich and dynamic visual experiences across various platforms and devices.

One of the primary functions of graphics and images in UI design is to enhance the visual appeal of the interface and establish a strong visual identity or brand presence. By selecting appropriate colors, shapes, and styles, designers can create cohesive and visually appealing interfaces that reflect the personality and values of the brand or product. Additionally, incorporating logos, icons, and other visual elements can help reinforce brand recognition and establish a consistent visual language across different screens and interactions.

To integrate graphics and images effectively into UI design, designers often use graphic design software such as Adobe Photoshop, Illustrator, or Sketch to create or manipulate visual assets. These tools provide a range of features and capabilities for designing graphics and images, including drawing tools, layer management, image editing, and export options. Designers can create custom graphics from scratch or modify existing images to align with the design aesthetics and requirements of the interface.

Once the graphics and images are created or prepared, designers can then integrate them into the UI using design tools or development frameworks. In web development, designers can use HTML and CSS to embed images directly into the HTML markup or apply them as background images to elements such as buttons, headers, or banners. By specifying the URL or file path of the image in the CSS stylesheet, designers can control the positioning, size, and appearance of the image within the layout.

htmlCopy code

```html
<div class="banner"> <img src="banner-image.jpg" alt="Banner Image"> </div>
```

cssCopy code

```css
.banner { background-image: url('banner-image.jpg'); background-size: cover; background-position: center; }
```

In addition to static images, designers can also incorporate dynamic graphics and animations into UI design to create more engaging and interactive experiences. With technologies such as CSS animations, SVG (Scalable Vector Graphics), and JavaScript libraries like GreenSock Animation Platform (GSAP) or Anime.js, designers can create animated effects, transitions, and visualizations that respond to user interactions or changes in the application state.

For example, designers can use CSS animations to animate the appearance of elements on scroll or hover, creating fluid and interactive transitions that draw users' attention and provide feedback. By defining keyframes and animation properties in the CSS stylesheet, designers can control the timing, duration, and easing of the animation to achieve the desired visual effect.

cssCopy code

```css
@keyframes fadeIn { from { opacity: 0; } to { opacity: 1; } } .element { animation: fadeIn 1s ease-out; }
```

Moreover, designers can leverage SVG graphics to create scalable and resolution-independent images that maintain crispness and clarity across different screen sizes and resolutions. SVG graphics are composed of vector shapes and paths, making them lightweight and flexible for use in responsive web design. Designers can create SVG illustrations, icons, or logos using graphic design software or online tools and then embed them directly into the HTML markup or CSS stylesheet.

htmlCopy code

```html
<svg width="100" height="100" viewBox="0 0 100 100"> <circle cx="50" cy="50" r="40" fill="blue" /> </svg>
```

cssCopy code

```css
.icon { background-image: url('icon.svg'); width: 100px; height: 100px; }
```

Furthermore, designers can explore the use of stock photos, illustrations, or multimedia content to enrich the visual storytelling and engagement within the interface. By selecting high-quality and relevant images that resonate with the target audience, designers can evoke emotions, convey messages, and create memorable experiences that leave a lasting impression.

To deploy these techniques effectively, designers should consider factors such as visual hierarchy, contrast, balance, and accessibility when integrating graphics and images into UI design. They should also optimize images for performance and load times by using appropriate file formats, compression techniques, and lazy loading strategies. By carefully planning and executing the integration of graphics and images, designers can elevate the overall visual appeal and effectiveness of the user interface, ultimately enhancing user satisfaction and engagement.

Techniques for custom graphics rendering play a pivotal role in creating visually compelling and interactive user interfaces. Custom graphics rendering involves the generation and manipulation of graphics primitives, such as lines, shapes, and textures, to create unique visual elements and effects that cannot be achieved with standard UI components. By leveraging advanced rendering techniques and technologies, designers and developers can create dynamic and immersive visual experiences that captivate users and enhance the overall usability and engagement of the interface.

One of the primary techniques for custom graphics rendering is vector graphics rendering, which involves representing images and graphics as mathematical equations and geometric primitives. Unlike raster graphics, which are composed of pixels and can lose quality when scaled or resized, vector graphics remain crisp and clear at any size, making them ideal for scalable and resolution-independent rendering. To render vector graphics in web development, designers and developers can use SVG (Scalable Vector Graphics), a markup language for describing two-dimensional graphics in XML format.

SVG graphics can be embedded directly into HTML documents using the <svg> element or included as external files and referenced using the <img> or <object> elements. Designers can create custom graphics and illustrations using graphic design software or online tools and then export them as SVG files for use in web development. By defining shapes, paths, and attributes within the SVG markup, designers can create intricate and detailed graphics that maintain clarity and sharpness across different screen sizes and resolutions.

htmlCopy code

```
<svg width="200" height="200"> <circle cx="100" cy="100" r="80" fill="blue" /> </svg>
```

Another technique for custom graphics rendering is canvas rendering, which involves drawing graphics and images directly onto an HTML <canvas> element using JavaScript. Unlike SVG, which defines graphics as markup elements that can be manipulated and styled using CSS, canvas rendering provides a low-level graphics API for programmatically rendering shapes, paths, and pixels on the canvas. Developers can use the canvas API to create interactive graphics, animations, and games that respond to user input and events.

To render graphics on a canvas element in web development, developers can use JavaScript to access the canvas context and draw shapes, paths, text, and images onto the canvas. By defining drawing operations within JavaScript functions and event handlers, developers can create dynamic and responsive graphics that update in real-time based on user interactions or changes in the application state. Additionally, developers can leverage libraries like PixiJS, Three.js, or D3.js to simplify complex rendering tasks and create visually stunning graphics and visualizations.

htmlCopy code

```
<canvas id="myCanvas" width="200" height="200"></canvas>
```

javascriptCopy code

```
const canvas = document.getElementById('myCanvas'); const ctx = canvas.getContext('2d'); ctx.fillStyle = 'blue'; ctx.beginPath(); ctx.arc(100, 100, 80, 0, 2 * Math.PI); ctx.fill();
```

In addition to vector graphics and canvas rendering, developers can also utilize WebGL (Web Graphics Library) for high-performance 3D graphics rendering in web applications. WebGL is a JavaScript API for rendering interactive 3D graphics within web browsers, leveraging the capabilities of the GPU (Graphics Processing Unit) to achieve hardware-accelerated rendering. With WebGL, developers can create immersive 3D environments, simulations, and visualizations that run smoothly and efficiently in modern web browsers.

To render 3D graphics with WebGL, developers typically use a combination of JavaScript, HTML, and GLSL (OpenGL Shading Language) to define and manipulate 3D objects, textures, lighting, and shaders. By writing custom shader programs in GLSL, developers can implement advanced rendering effects such as lighting, shadows, reflections, and post-processing effects. WebGL frameworks and libraries like Three.js provide abstractions and utilities for working with WebGL, making it easier for developers to create complex 3D scenes and animations.

htmlCopy code

```html
<script src="https://cdnjs.cloudflare.com/ajax/libs/three.js/r128/three.min.js"></script> <script> const scene = new THREE.Scene(); const camera = new THREE.PerspectiveCamera(75, window.innerWidth / window.innerHeight, 0.1, 1000); const renderer = new THREE.WebGLRenderer();
renderer.setSize(window.innerWidth, window.innerHeight);
document.body.appendChild(renderer.domElement); const geometry = new THREE.BoxGeometry(); const material = new THREE.MeshBasicMaterial({ color: 0x00ff00 }); const cube = new THREE.Mesh(geometry, material); scene.add(cube); camera.position.z = 5; function animate() { requestAnimationFrame(animate); cube.rotation.x += 0.01; cube.rotation.y += 0.01; renderer.render(scene, camera); } animate(); </script>
```

In summary, techniques for custom graphics rendering offer designers and developers powerful tools for creating visually stunning and interactive user interfaces. Whether using vector graphics, canvas rendering, or WebGL, designers and developers can leverage advanced rendering techniques to create unique visual experiences that engage users and enhance the overall usability and appeal of the interface. By mastering these techniques and exploring creative possibilities, designers and developers can push the boundaries of UI design and deliver memorable and impactful user experiences.

Chapter 7: Creating Dynamic UI Elements with Delphi Pascal

Generating UI elements programmatically is a fundamental aspect of software development, enabling developers to dynamically create and manipulate user interface components based on application logic and data. This approach offers flexibility and scalability, allowing developers to build complex and responsive interfaces that adapt to changing requirements and user interactions. By generating UI elements programmatically, developers can streamline development workflows, improve code maintainability, and achieve greater control over the appearance and behavior of the interface.

In web development, generating UI elements programmatically often involves using JavaScript to manipulate the DOM (Document Object Model) dynamically. The DOM represents the structure of an HTML document as a hierarchical tree of nodes, and developers can use JavaScript to access and modify these nodes to create or update UI elements in response to user actions or application events. By selecting parent elements, creating new elements, and appending or inserting them into the DOM, developers can generate UI elements on the fly, without relying on static HTML markup.

javascriptCopy code

```
// Select the parent element const parentElement =
document.getElementById('container'); // Create a
new element const newElement =
document.createElement('div'); // Set properties and
attributes newElement.textContent = 'Dynamic UI
Element'; newElement.classList.add('dynamic-
element'); // Append the new element to the parent
parentElement.appendChild(newElement);
```

Similarly, in desktop and mobile application
development, generating UI elements programmatically
involves using platform-specific APIs or frameworks to
create and manage UI components dynamically. For
example, in iOS development using Swift, developers
can use UIKit to programmatically create and configure
UI elements such as views, buttons, labels, and text
fields. By instantiating and customizing UI components
in code, developers can define their appearance, layout,
and behavior programmatically, giving them precise
control over the user interface.

swiftCopy code

```
// Create a new UILabel instance let label = UILabel()
// Set label properties label.text = "Dynamic UI
Element" label.textAlignment = .center label.textColor
= .black // Add label to the view hierarchy
view.addSubview(label)
```

Similarly, in Android development using Java or Kotlin,
developers can use the Android SDK to
programmatically create and manipulate UI elements
within activities or fragments. By instantiating view

objects such as TextView, Button, or ImageView, and configuring their properties and attributes programmatically, developers can dynamically generate UI elements and customize their appearance and behavior based on application logic or user preferences.

javaCopy code

```
// Create a new TextView instance TextView textView
= new TextView(context); // Set TextView properties
textView.setText("Dynamic    UI    Element");
textView.setTextColor(Color.BLACK);
textView.setTextSize(TypedValue.COMPLEX_UNIT_SP,
16); // Add TextView to the layout
layout.addView(textView);
```

In addition to creating individual UI elements programmatically, developers can also generate UI layouts dynamically by combining multiple elements and arranging them in containers or layout managers. By nesting view or layout objects within one another and specifying their relationships and constraints, developers can create complex and responsive UI layouts that adapt to different screen sizes and orientations. This approach allows developers to design flexible and scalable user interfaces that maintain consistency and usability across various devices and form factors.

javaCopy code

```
// Create a LinearLayout instance LinearLayout
linearLayout = new LinearLayout(context);
linearLayout.setOrientation(LinearLayout.VERTICAL); //
Create TextView instances TextView textView1 = new
```

```
TextView(context); TextView textView2 = new
TextView(context); // Set TextView properties
textView1.setText("Dynamic UI Element 1");
textView2.setText("Dynamic UI Element 2"); // Add
TextViews to the LinearLayout
linearLayout.addView(textView1);
linearLayout.addView(textView2); // Add the
LinearLayout to the parent layout
parentLayout.addView(linearLayout);
```

Moreover, generating UI elements programmatically enables developers to implement dynamic UI patterns such as data-driven UI, where UI elements are generated dynamically based on data retrieved from a backend server or local database. By fetching data asynchronously and populating UI elements dynamically, developers can create data-driven interfaces that display real-time information and respond to user inputs or updates dynamically. This approach allows developers to build interactive and data-rich applications that deliver a seamless user experience.

In summary, generating UI elements programmatically is a powerful technique that empowers developers to create dynamic, responsive, and data-driven user interfaces across various platforms and technologies. By leveraging platform-specific APIs, frameworks, and programming languages, developers can programmatically create, customize, and manage UI components, enabling them to build flexible, scalable, and engaging applications that meet the evolving needs of users and businesses. Through careful design and implementation, developers can harness the full potential of programmatically generated UI elements to deliver impactful and intuitive user experiences.

Dynamically adjusting the user interface (UI) based on user input is a crucial aspect of modern application development, allowing applications to provide personalized and responsive experiences tailored to individual user preferences and interactions. This technique involves detecting and interpreting user input, such as clicks, taps, keystrokes, or gestures, and dynamically updating the UI elements, layout, content, or behavior in real-time to reflect the user's actions or choices. By dynamically adjusting the UI based on user input, developers can enhance usability, streamline workflows, and improve overall user satisfaction.

In web development, dynamically adjusting the UI based on user input often involves using JavaScript to listen for DOM events triggered by user interactions and updating the DOM dynamically in response. For example, developers can attach event listeners to form elements such as text fields, checkboxes, or dropdown menus to detect changes in their values or states. When a user interacts with these elements, such as typing text into a text field or selecting an option from a dropdown menu, the corresponding event is fired, and developers can handle it by updating other UI elements accordingly.

javascriptCopy code

```
// Listen for changes in a text field const textField =
document.getElementById('text-field');
textField.addEventListener('input', (event) => { //
Update UI based on user input const inputValue =
event.target.value; // Dynamically update other UI
elements updateUI(inputValue); });
```

Similarly, in desktop and mobile application development, dynamically adjusting the UI based on user input involves responding to user interactions with UI controls or widgets. For example, in iOS development using Swift, developers can implement delegate methods or target-action mechanisms to handle user input events generated by UI controls such as buttons, sliders, or text fields. By defining callback functions or closures to handle user input events, developers can update the UI elements or trigger specific actions based on the user's interactions.

swiftCopy code

```
// Define a target-action method for a button
@IBAction func buttonTapped(_ sender: UIButton) {
// Update UI based on user input updateUI() }
```

Similarly, in Android development using Java or Kotlin, developers can use event listeners or callback interfaces to respond to user input events generated by UI components such as buttons, EditText fields, or RecyclerView items. By registering event listeners and implementing callback methods, developers can capture user interactions and update the UI dynamically to reflect changes in the application state or user preferences.

```java
javaCopy code
// Define an OnClickListener for a button  Button
button           =           findViewById(R.id.button);
button.setOnClickListener( new   View.OnClickListener()
{ @Override  public  void  onClick(View v) { // Update
UI based on user input  updateUI(); } });
```

One common use case for dynamically adjusting the UI based on user input is form validation, where developers validate user input in real-time as users fill out input fields in a form. By monitoring changes to form fields and applying validation rules, developers can provide immediate feedback to users about the validity of their input and prevent submission of invalid data. This approach helps improve the user experience by reducing errors and guiding users through the input process more smoothly.

Another use case is dynamic content loading, where developers fetch and display additional content or data based on user interactions such as scrolling, clicking, or tapping. For example, in web development, developers can implement infinite scrolling or pagination techniques to load more content as users scroll down a webpage or navigate through paginated results. By dynamically loading content in response to user input, developers can optimize performance and enhance usability by presenting relevant information on demand. Furthermore, dynamically adjusting the UI based on user input enables developers to implement interactive features such as autocomplete suggestions, live search functionality, or context-aware menus. By analyzing user input and predicting user intent, developers can offer suggestions, refine search results, or present relevant options dynamically, making the user experience more efficient and intuitive.

In summary, dynamically adjusting the UI based on user input is a fundamental technique in application development, allowing developers to create responsive, interactive, and user-centric interfaces. By listening for user interactions and updating the UI dynamically in response, developers can tailor the user experience to individual preferences, streamline workflows, and improve overall usability and satisfaction. Through careful design and implementation, developers can leverage this technique to build applications that engage users, facilitate task completion, and deliver seamless and enjoyable user experiences.

Chapter 8: Enhancing User Experience with Animation and Effects

Adding animation effects to UI components is a powerful technique in modern application development, enhancing user experience by adding visual appeal, interactivity, and engagement to the user interface. Animation effects can range from subtle transitions and fades to more complex animations such as movement, scaling, rotation, and morphing. By incorporating animation effects strategically, developers can create dynamic and polished interfaces that captivate users, convey feedback, and communicate information effectively.

In web development, adding animation effects to UI components often involves using CSS (Cascading Style Sheets) or JavaScript to define and control animations. CSS provides built-in support for keyframe animations and transitions, allowing developers to create simple animations with ease. By defining animation properties such as duration, timing function, delay, and iteration count, developers can customize the behavior and appearance of animations to suit the design requirements and user experience goals.

cssCopy code

```
/* Define a CSS animation */ @keyframes fadeIn {
from { opacity: 0; } to { opacity: 1; } } /* Apply the
```

animation to a UI component */ .element {
animation-name: fadeln; animation-duration: 1s;
animation-delay: 0.5s; animation-fill-mode:
forwards; /* Maintain final state after animation */ }
Additionally, developers can use CSS transitions to
create smooth and gradual changes in UI component
properties such as color, size, position, and opacity.
By specifying transition properties and durations for
specific CSS properties, developers can define how
changes to those properties are animated when
triggered by user interactions or changes in the
application state.

cssCopy code

```
/* Define a CSS transition */ .element { transition-
property: background-color, transform; transition-
duration: 0.3s; transition-timing-function: ease-in-
out; } /* Apply the transition to a UI component */
.element:hover { background-color: #ff0000;
transform: scale(1.1); }
```

In addition to CSS, developers can use JavaScript
libraries and frameworks such as GSAP (GreenSock
Animation Platform) or Anime.js to create more
complex and interactive animations in web
applications. These libraries provide advanced
features and controls for animating UI components,
including support for timelines, sequences, easing
functions, and event-based triggers. By leveraging
JavaScript animation libraries, developers can create

sophisticated animations with precise control over timing, sequencing, and choreography, enabling them to implement engaging and immersive user experiences.

javascriptCopy code

```
// Using GSAP to animate a UI component
gsap.to('.element', { duration: 1, x: 100, rotation: 360, ease: 'power2.out' });
```

Similarly, in desktop and mobile application development, adding animation effects to UI components involves using platform-specific APIs or frameworks to create and control animations. For example, in iOS development using Swift, developers can use Core Animation to create animations for UI components such as views, layers, and transitions. By defining animation objects and specifying animation properties such as duration, timing function, and keyframes, developers can create fluid and responsive animations that enhance the user experience.

swiftCopy code

```
// Using Core Animation to animate a UIView
UIView.animate(withDuration: 0.5, delay: 0, options: .curveEaseInOut, animations: { self.view.transform = CGAffineTransform(rotationAngle: CGFloat.pi) }, completion: nil)
```

Similarly, in Android development using Java or Kotlin, developers can use the Android Animation API to create animations for UI components such as views, layouts, and drawable objects. By defining animation resources or programmatically creating animation objects, developers can animate UI components with effects such as translation, rotation, scaling, and alpha fading, enhancing the visual appeal and usability of the application.

javaCopy code

```
// Using Android Animation API to animate a View
Animation animation = AnimationUtils.loadAnimation(context,
R.anim.slide_in_left);
view.startAnimation(animation);
```

One common use case for adding animation effects to UI components is providing visual feedback to users in response to their interactions with the application. For example, animating button presses, menu selections, or form submissions can provide immediate feedback to users, indicating that their actions have been recognized and processed by the application. This feedback helps improve the responsiveness and perceived performance of the application, enhancing the overall user experience.

Another use case is guiding users' attention and focus within the application interface by animating UI elements strategically. By animating important UI elements or transitions between different states or screens, developers can draw users' attention to key features, actions, or content areas, helping them navigate the interface more efficiently and intuitively. This technique can be particularly useful for onboarding experiences, tutorials, or walkthroughs, where guiding users' attention is essential for effective communication and engagement.

In summary, adding animation effects to UI components is a valuable technique in application development, allowing developers to enhance user experience, improve usability, and communicate effectively with users. Whether using CSS animations, JavaScript libraries, or platform-specific APIs, developers can leverage animation to create dynamic and engaging interfaces that delight users and elevate the overall quality of the application. By incorporating animation strategically and thoughtfully, developers can transform static UI components into dynamic and interactive elements that captivate users and leave a lasting impression.

Improving user interaction with visual feedback is a pivotal aspect of user interface (UI) design and application development, playing a crucial role in enhancing user experience, usability, and overall satisfaction. Visual feedback refers to the visual cues, animations, or changes in UI elements that occur in response to user actions, interactions, or system events, providing users with immediate and meaningful feedback about their interactions with the application. By incorporating visual feedback effectively, developers can create interfaces that are more intuitive, engaging, and responsive, ultimately leading to a more enjoyable and productive user experience.

One common way to improve user interaction with visual feedback is by providing immediate feedback to user actions, such as button clicks, menu selections, or form submissions. When a user interacts with a UI element, such as clicking a button or tapping a link, the application should respond promptly with visual feedback, indicating that the action has been recognized and processed. This feedback can take various forms, such as changing the appearance of the UI element, displaying a loading indicator, or triggering an animation or transition, depending on the context and nature of the interaction.

javascriptCopy code

```javascript
// Example of providing immediate feedback with JavaScript const button = document.getElementById('submit-button');
button.addEventListener('click', () => { // Display a loading spinner while processing the action button.classList.add('loading');       // Simulate processing time setTimeout(() => { // Remove the loading spinner and display success message button.classList.remove('loading');
button.classList.add('success'); }, 2000); });
```

Additionally, visual feedback can be used to communicate the outcome of user actions or system events, such as successful completion of a task, error or validation messages, or status updates. By presenting feedback in a clear and visually distinctive manner, such as using color-coded messages, icons, or tooltips, developers can convey important information to users effectively, reducing ambiguity and confusion. This helps users understand the outcome of their actions and make informed decisions, leading to a smoother and more efficient user experience.

htmlCopy code

```
<!-- Example of displaying status feedback with HTML/CSS --> <div class="message success"> <i class="fas fa-check-circle"></i> Task completed successfully! </div>
```

Moreover, visual feedback can be used to guide users' attention and focus within the interface, drawing attention to important UI elements, features, or content areas. Techniques such as highlighting, animation, or contrast can be employed to make critical elements stand out visually, helping users navigate the interface more easily and accomplish their tasks more efficiently. By guiding users' attention strategically, developers can ensure that users remain engaged and focused on the most relevant aspects of the application, enhancing usability and user satisfaction.

cssCopy code

```
/* Example of highlighting important UI elements with CSS */ .button-primary { background-color: #007bff; /* Blue */ color: #fff; /* White */
```

transition: background-color 0.3s ease; } .button-primary:hover { background-color: #0056b3; /* Darker blue on hover */ }

Furthermore, visual feedback can be used to provide context-sensitive assistance or hints to users as they interact with the application. Techniques such as tooltips, hints, or interactive tutorials can be employed to provide users with additional information or guidance about specific UI elements or features, helping them understand their functionality or purpose. By offering contextual assistance in real-time, developers can empower users to navigate the interface more confidently and perform tasks more effectively, leading to a more positive and rewarding user experience.

javascriptCopy code

```javascript
// Example of displaying tooltips with JavaScript
const tooltipTrigger = document.getElementById('tooltip-trigger'); const tooltipContent = document.getElementById('tooltip-content');
tooltipTrigger.addEventListener('mouseover', () => {
// Show tooltip content tooltipContent.style.display = 'block'; });
tooltipTrigger.addEventListener('mouseout', () => {
// Hide tooltip content tooltipContent.style.display = 'none'; });
```

In summary, improving user interaction with visual feedback is essential for creating engaging, intuitive, and user-friendly interfaces in applications. By providing immediate feedback to user actions, communicating outcomes effectively, guiding users' attention, and offering contextual assistance, developers can enhance the usability, efficiency, and overall quality of the user experience. Through thoughtful design and implementation of visual feedback mechanisms, developers can create interfaces that not only meet users' needs and expectations but also delight and empower them to achieve their goals effectively.

Chapter 9: Responsive Design Principles for Delphi Applications

Designing user interfaces (UIs) for various screen resolutions is a fundamental aspect of modern application development, essential for ensuring that applications are accessible and usable across a wide range of devices, displays, and platforms. With the proliferation of smartphones, tablets, laptops, desktops, and other devices with diverse screen sizes and resolutions, developers face the challenge of creating UIs that adapt seamlessly to different screen dimensions while maintaining consistency, usability, and visual appeal. By adopting responsive design principles, flexible layout techniques, and adaptive UI components, developers can create UIs that provide an optimal viewing and interaction experience for users on any device or screen resolution.

One key aspect of designing UIs for various screen resolutions is adopting a responsive design approach, which involves designing UI layouts that automatically adjust and adapt to different screen sizes and orientations. Responsive design techniques typically rely on CSS media queries to apply different styles based on the screen width, allowing developers to create fluid and flexible layouts that can accommodate a wide range of devices and viewport sizes. By using relative units such as percentages, ems, or viewport units, developers can create UIs that scale proportionally and maintain their usability and readability across different screen resolutions.

cssCopy code

```
/* Example of using media queries for responsive design */ @media screen and (max-width: 768px) { .container { width: 100%; } } @media screen and (min-width: 768px) { .container { width: 768px; } }
```

Another important consideration in designing UIs for various screen resolutions is ensuring that UI components and content are appropriately sized and spaced to accommodate different screen densities and pixel densities. High-density displays, such as Retina displays on Apple devices, have a higher pixel density, requiring UI elements to be rendered at higher resolutions to maintain sharpness and clarity. Developers can use CSS techniques such as device pixel ratios and image resolution switching to serve high-resolution assets to devices with high-density displays, ensuring that UIs look crisp and visually appealing across different screen resolutions.

cssCopy code

```
/* Example of serving high-resolution images with CSS */ @media screen and (-webkit-min-device-pixel-ratio: 2), screen and (min-resolution: 192dpi) { .logo { background-image: url('logo@2x.png'); background-size: contain; } }
```

Additionally, developers can leverage adaptive UI components and design patterns to create UIs that gracefully degrade or adapt to different screen sizes and resolutions. Adaptive UI components, such as flexible grids, fluid layouts, and scalable icons, can adjust their appearance and behavior dynamically based on the available screen space, ensuring that UIs remain usable and functional regardless of the device or viewport size. By prioritizing content hierarchy, minimizing clutter, and focusing on essential elements, developers can create UIs that prioritize usability and readability, even on smaller screens or lower resolutions.

One common technique for designing UIs for various screen resolutions is the use of breakpoints, which are specific screen widths at which the layout or appearance of the UI changes to accommodate different screen sizes. By defining breakpoints based on common device categories or viewport dimensions, developers can create responsive designs that adapt smoothly across a spectrum of devices, from smartphones and tablets to desktop computers and large-screen displays. Breakpoints allow developers to optimize the layout, typography, and navigation of the UI at different screen sizes, ensuring that users have a consistent and optimal experience regardless of their device or screen resolution.

cssCopy code

```
/* Example of defining breakpoints for responsive
design */ @media screen and (max-width: 576px) {
/* Styles for small screens (e.g., smartphones) */ }
@media screen and (min-width: 576px) and (max-
width: 992px) { /* Styles for medium screens (e.g.,
tablets) */ } @media screen and (min-width: 992px)
and (max-width: 1200px) { /* Styles for large screens
```

(e.g., laptops) */ } @media screen and (min-width: 1200px) { /* Styles for extra-large screens (e.g., desktops) */ }

Furthermore, developers can leverage modern CSS features such as Flexbox and CSS Grid Layout to create more complex and dynamic layouts that adapt fluidly to different screen resolutions. Flexbox provides a flexible and efficient way to distribute space and align items within a container, making it ideal for creating responsive layouts with variable content and screen sizes. CSS Grid Layout offers a powerful grid-based layout system that enables developers to create complex, multi-column layouts with ease, allowing for greater control over the arrangement and alignment of UI components across different screen resolutions.

cssCopy code

```css
/* Example of using Flexbox for responsive layout */
.container { display: flex; flex-direction: column; justify-content: center; align-items: center; }
```

In summary, designing UIs for various screen resolutions requires a combination of responsive design techniques, adaptive UI components, and careful consideration of user needs and preferences across different devices and platforms. By adopting a responsive design approach, leveraging adaptive UI components, defining breakpoints, and using modern CSS features, developers can create UIs that are visually appealing, user-friendly, and accessible on devices of all sizes and resolutions. Through thoughtful design and implementation, developers can ensure that their applications provide a consistent and optimal user experience across the diverse landscape of devices and screen resolutions.

Implementing adaptive layouts for different devices is crucial in today's digital landscape, where users access applications from a variety of devices with varying screen sizes, resolutions, and orientations. An adaptive layout dynamically adjusts its design and structure based on the characteristics of the device being used, ensuring optimal presentation and usability across a range of screen sizes and form factors. By employing adaptive layout techniques, developers can create user interfaces that provide a consistent and intuitive experience, regardless of the device being used.

One fundamental aspect of implementing adaptive layouts is utilizing media queries in CSS to target specific device characteristics, such as screen width, height, orientation, and pixel density. Media queries allow developers to apply different stylesheets or style rules based on the device's features, enabling them to tailor the layout and design for optimal viewing on various devices. By defining breakpoints within media queries, developers can adjust the layout at specific screen sizes, ensuring that content is displayed appropriately and effectively across different devices.

cssCopy code

```
/* Example of using media queries for adaptive layouts */ @media screen and (max-width: 768px) { /* Styles for small screens (e.g., smartphones) */ } @media screen and (min-width: 768px) and (max-width:
```

1024px) { /* Styles for medium screens (e.g., tablets) */ } @media screen and (min-width: 1024px) { /* Styles for large screens (e.g., laptops and desktops) */ }

Another effective technique for implementing adaptive layouts is employing flexible or fluid grid systems, such as CSS Grid Layout or Flexbox, to create layouts that can adapt dynamically to different screen sizes and aspect ratios. These grid systems enable developers to define flexible layouts that adjust automatically based on available space, allowing content to reflow and rearrange smoothly as the viewport size changes. By using relative units like percentages or viewport units, developers can create layouts that scale proportionally to fit the screen, ensuring a consistent and visually pleasing experience across devices.

cssCopy code

```css
/* Example of using Flexbox for adaptive layouts */
.container { display: flex; flex-direction: column; justify-content: center; align-items: center; }
```

In addition to responsive design techniques, developers can also leverage device detection libraries or server-side techniques to customize the layout and functionality based on the specific characteristics of the user's device. Device detection allows developers to identify the type of device accessing the application, such as a smartphone, tablet, or desktop computer, and serve tailored content or features accordingly. By detecting device attributes like screen size, resolution, and input capabilities, developers can optimize the layout and user experience for each device category, ensuring that users receive the most appropriate and optimized version of the application.

javascriptCopy code

```javascript
// Example of using JavaScript for device detection if (window.innerWidth < 768) { // Load mobile-specific layout and features } else if (window.innerWidth >= 768 && window.innerWidth < 1024) { // Load tablet-specific layout and features } else { // Load desktop-specific layout and features }
```

Furthermore, developers can enhance adaptive layouts by incorporating touch-friendly interactions and gestures for touchscreen devices, such as swiping, tapping, and pinch-to-zoom gestures. Touch-friendly UI elements, larger tap targets, and intuitive navigation patterns can improve the usability and accessibility of the application on touchscreen devices, providing a seamless and intuitive experience for users interacting via touch input. By designing with touch in mind and optimizing interactions for touchscreens, developers can create adaptive layouts that cater to the growing number of mobile and tablet users.

cssCopy code

```css
/* Example of using CSS for touch-friendly styles */
.button { /* Increase padding and font size for easier tapping */ padding: 10px 20px; font-size: 16px; }
```

In summary, implementing adaptive layouts for different devices is essential for delivering a consistent, user-friendly experience across the diverse range of devices and screen sizes used by modern users. By utilizing responsive design techniques, flexible grid systems, device detection, and touch-friendly interactions, developers can create adaptive layouts that seamlessly adapt to the unique characteristics of each device, providing users with an optimal viewing and interaction experience. Through thoughtful design and implementation, developers can ensure that their applications are accessible, usable, and visually appealing across all devices, enhancing user satisfaction and engagement.

Chapter 10: Advanced Visual Designing Techniques and Patterns

Applying design patterns to UI development is a fundamental practice for creating scalable, maintainable, and efficient user interfaces. Design patterns are proven solutions to common problems encountered during software development, offering developers a blueprint for structuring their code and organizing their UI components in a logical and reusable manner. By leveraging design patterns, developers can streamline the UI development process, improve code readability and maintainability, and ensure consistency and coherence across their applications.

One widely used design pattern in UI development is the Model-View-Controller (MVC) pattern, which separates the application's data (model), presentation logic (view), and user interaction (controller) into distinct components. The MVC pattern promotes modularity, flexibility, and reusability by decoupling the UI from the underlying data and business logic, allowing developers to make changes to one component without affecting the others. In MVC, the model represents the data and business logic, the view represents the presentation layer, and the controller handles user input and updates the model and view accordingly.

pythonCopy code

```
# Example of applying MVC pattern in Python Flask framework from flask import Flask, render_template
```

```python
app = Flask(__name__) @app.route('/') def index(): #
Model: Data retrieval from database data =
retrieve_data_from_database() # View: Rendering
HTML template with data return
render_template('index.html',                data=data)
@app.route('/update',      methods=['POST'])      def
update(): # Controller: Handling user input and
updating data new_data = request.form['new_data']
update_data_in_database(new_data)              return
redirect('/')
```

Another commonly used design pattern in UI
development is the Observer pattern, which facilitates
communication and synchronization between UI
components by establishing a one-to-many relationship
between subjects (observed) and observers (listeners).
In the Observer pattern, when the state of the subject
changes, it notifies all registered observers, allowing
them to react and update their state accordingly. This
pattern is particularly useful for implementing event-
driven architectures and handling asynchronous
updates in UIs.

javascriptCopy code

```javascript
// Example of applying Observer pattern in JavaScript
class Subject { constructor() { this.observers = []; }
addObserver(observer)                                 {
this.observers.push(observer); } notifyObservers() {
this.observers.forEach(observer                     =>
observer.update()); } } class Observer { update() { //
Handle UI update logic } } // Usage const subject =
```

new Subject(); const observer1 = new Observer();
const observer2 = new Observer();
subject.addObserver(observer1);
subject.addObserver(observer2); // When the state of
the subject changes subject.notifyObservers();
Additionally, design patterns such as the Factory
pattern, Singleton pattern, and Decorator pattern can
be applied to UI development to address specific
requirements and challenges. The Factory pattern
facilitates the creation of complex UI components by
encapsulating the instantiation logic and providing a
centralized factory class responsible for creating
instances of different UI elements. The Singleton
pattern ensures that only one instance of a particular UI
component exists throughout the application, useful for
managing global resources and state. The Decorator
pattern allows developers to dynamically extend or
modify the behavior of UI components by wrapping
them with additional functionality.

javaCopy code

```
// Example of applying Factory pattern in Java Swing
framework public class UIFactory { public static
UIComponent createUIComponent(String type) { if
(type.equals("button")) { return new Button(); } else
if (type.equals("textbox")) { return new TextBox(); }
else { throw new IllegalArgumentException("Invalid
UI component type"); } } }
```

In summary, applying design patterns to UI
development enables developers to build robust,

maintainable, and scalable user interfaces by leveraging established best practices and solutions to common problems. By adopting patterns such as MVC, Observer, Factory, Singleton, and Decorator, developers can improve code organization, modularity, and reusability, resulting in more efficient development workflows and higher-quality UIs. Through thoughtful application of design patterns, developers can create UIs that are easier to understand, extend, and maintain, ultimately leading to better user experiences and increased productivity.

Optimizing visual design for performance and scalability is essential in ensuring that user interfaces deliver a smooth and responsive experience, particularly in modern web and mobile applications where users expect fast load times and seamless interactions. While visual design is primarily concerned with aesthetics and usability, it also plays a significant role in determining the performance and scalability of an application. By employing various optimization techniques and best practices, developers and designers can create visually appealing interfaces that perform efficiently and scale effectively across different devices and usage scenarios.
One key aspect of optimizing visual design for performance is minimizing the size and complexity of assets, such as images, icons, and graphics, used in the UI. Large or uncompressed assets can significantly increase page load times and consume excessive bandwidth, especially on mobile devices with limited network connectivity. To address this issue, developers

can employ compression techniques, such as image optimization and sprite sheets, to reduce file sizes without compromising visual quality. Additionally, using vector graphics formats like SVG (Scalable Vector Graphics) can help maintain sharpness and clarity across different screen resolutions while keeping file sizes minimal.

bashCopy code

```
# Example of CLI command to optimize images using ImageMagick convert input.jpg -resize 50% output.jpg # Example of CLI command to compress images using JPEGoptim jpegoptim --max=80 input.jpg
```

Another important consideration for optimizing visual design is reducing the number of HTTP requests required to render the UI. Each HTTP request adds latency to the page load process, particularly on mobile networks where network latency is higher. To minimize the number of requests, developers can consolidate and combine CSS and JavaScript files into a single bundle using tools like webpack or Gulp. Additionally, utilizing CSS sprites for combining multiple images into a single image file reduces the number of image requests, resulting in faster load times and improved performance.

bashCopy code

```
# Example of CLI command to bundle CSS and JavaScript files using webpack webpack --config webpack.config.js # Example of CLI command to generate CSS sprites using SpriteSmith spritesmith --src assets/icons/*.png --out assets/spritesheet.png
```

Furthermore, optimizing the layout and structure of UI components can significantly improve rendering performance, especially on devices with limited processing power or memory. Complex layouts, nested elements, and excessive use of CSS animations or transitions can cause rendering bottlenecks and lead to sluggish performance. To address this, developers should prioritize simplicity and efficiency in their designs, avoiding unnecessary elements and effects that could impact performance. Using CSS flexbox or grid layouts instead of traditional float-based layouts can also improve rendering performance and facilitate responsive design.

cssCopy code

```css
/* Example of using CSS flexbox for efficient layout */
.container { display: flex; flex-direction: row; justify-content: space-between; }
```

Additionally, optimizing visual assets for lazy loading can further enhance performance by deferring the loading of non-critical resources until they are needed. Lazy loading techniques, such as Intersection Observer or scroll-based loading, allow developers to prioritize the loading of visible content while deferring the loading of off-screen or below-the-fold elements. This approach reduces initial page load times and conserves bandwidth, particularly for content-heavy applications with large images or media files.

javascriptCopy code

```javascript
// Example of implementing lazy loading using Intersection Observer API const observer = new
```

```
IntersectionObserver(entries        =>        {
entries.forEach(entry => { if (entry.isIntersecting) {
const img = entry.target; img.src = img.dataset.src;
observer.unobserve(img);         }        });        });
document.querySelectorAll('img.lazy').forEach(img =>
{ observer.observe(img); });
```

In summary, optimizing visual design for performance and scalability is crucial for delivering fast, responsive, and user-friendly interfaces in modern web and mobile applications. By minimizing asset sizes, reducing HTTP requests, optimizing layout structures, and implementing lazy loading techniques, developers and designers can create visually compelling interfaces that load quickly and scale seamlessly across different devices and usage scenarios. By incorporating these optimization strategies into the design and development process, teams can ensure that their applications provide an optimal user experience while maintaining high performance and scalability.

BOOK 3
ADVANCED TECHNIQUES IN DELPHI PASCAL:
INTEGRATED DEBUGGING STRATEGIES

ROB BOTWRIGHT

Chapter 1: Introduction to Debugging in Delphi Pascal

The importance of debugging in software development cannot be overstated. Debugging is the process of identifying and resolving defects, errors, or unexpected behavior in software applications, and it plays a critical role in ensuring the reliability, functionality, and quality of software products. While software development strives for perfection, bugs and issues inevitably arise during the development process, whether due to human error, complexity of code, or unforeseen interactions between different components. Therefore, effective debugging techniques and practices are essential for developers to diagnose and rectify problems efficiently, minimizing the impact on users and maintaining the integrity of the software.

One of the primary reasons debugging is crucial in software development is its role in ensuring the functionality and correctness of applications. Even minor bugs or glitches can have significant consequences, ranging from inconveniencing users to causing system failures or data loss. By thoroughly debugging their code, developers can identify and fix issues before they escalate into more serious problems, thereby enhancing the reliability and usability of their software. Moreover, debugging helps validate that the software behaves as intended, meeting the requirements and expectations of stakeholders and end users.

bashCopy code

```
# Example of debugging command in Python using pdb python -m pdb script.py
```

Additionally, debugging is essential for optimizing the performance and efficiency of software applications. Performance bottlenecks, memory leaks, and inefficient algorithms can degrade the responsiveness and scalability of applications, leading to poor user experience and increased resource consumption. Through systematic debugging and profiling, developers can pinpoint areas of code that contribute to performance issues and implement optimizations to enhance speed, responsiveness, and resource utilization. By addressing performance-related issues early in the development cycle, developers can ensure that their software meets performance requirements and delivers optimal performance under varying conditions.

bashCopy code

```
# Example of profiling command in Python using cProfile python -m cProfile script.py
```

Moreover, debugging fosters continuous learning and improvement among developers. The process of diagnosing and solving problems requires critical thinking, problem-solving skills, and attention to detail, which are essential qualities for effective software development. By encountering and overcoming challenges through debugging, developers gain valuable experience and insights that contribute to their growth and proficiency as software engineers. Additionally, debugging encourages collaboration and knowledge sharing within development teams, as developers often collaborate to diagnose and resolve complex issues, leveraging each other's expertise and perspectives to find solutions.

bashCopy code

Example of debugging command in JavaScript using Node.js debugger node inspect script.js

Furthermore, debugging plays a crucial role in maintaining software quality and reducing technical debt. Technical debt refers to the accumulation of incomplete or suboptimal code, often resulting from shortcuts taken during development or deferred maintenance of code. Left unresolved, technical debt can impede future development efforts, increase the likelihood of introducing new bugs, and hinder the long-term maintainability of the software. By actively debugging and refactoring code to address underlying issues and improve code quality, developers can mitigate technical debt, streamline development workflows, and ensure the sustainability of their software projects.

bashCopy code

Example of debugging command in Java using jdb jdb MyClass

In summary, debugging is an indispensable aspect of software development, encompassing various techniques, tools, and practices aimed at identifying, diagnosing, and resolving issues in software applications. From ensuring functionality and correctness to optimizing performance, fostering learning and collaboration, and maintaining software quality, debugging plays a multifaceted role in the development lifecycle. By prioritizing effective debugging practices and integrating debugging workflows into their development processes, developers can build robust, reliable, and high-quality software products that meet the needs and expectations of users and stakeholders.

The debugging process in Delphi is a crucial aspect of software development, enabling developers to identify and rectify errors, defects, and unexpected behavior in their applications. With Delphi's powerful integrated development environment (IDE) and comprehensive debugging tools, developers can effectively diagnose and resolve issues, ensuring the reliability, functionality, and quality of their Delphi applications. The debugging process in Delphi typically involves several key steps, starting with the identification of the problem and proceeding through the analysis, diagnosis, and resolution stages. One of the initial steps in the debugging process is to reproduce the issue or problem encountered in the application. By replicating the conditions or actions that trigger the issue, developers can gain insights into its underlying cause and behavior, facilitating the debugging process.

bashCopy code

Example of setting a breakpoint in Delphi IDE F9

Once the issue has been reproduced, developers can leverage Delphi's debugging tools to inspect the state of the application and analyze its behavior. Delphi provides various debugging features, including breakpoints, watch lists, and variable inspection, which allow developers to pause the execution of their code at specific points and examine the values of variables, objects, and expressions. By strategically placing breakpoints at critical junctures in the code and stepping through the program's execution, developers can gain visibility into the flow of control and identify anomalies or unexpected behavior.

bashCopy code

Example of adding a watch expression in Delphi IDE Ctrl + F5

Furthermore, Delphi's debugging tools offer real-time insights into the runtime behavior of applications, enabling developers to track the execution of their code and monitor changes to variables and objects as they occur. By observing the sequence of operations and interactions between different components, developers can pinpoint the source of errors or discrepancies and formulate hypotheses about their root causes. Additionally, Delphi's call stack and event log features provide valuable contextual information about the sequence of function calls and events leading up to the occurrence of the issue, aiding developers in tracing the execution path and identifying potential points of failure.

bashCopy code

Example of accessing the call stack in Delphi IDE Alt + C

Once the issue has been analyzed and diagnosed, developers can proceed with the resolution stage of the debugging process, where they implement corrective actions to address the identified problems. Depending on the nature of the issue, resolutions may involve modifying code logic, correcting syntax errors, or adjusting configuration settings. Delphi's integrated development environment provides a seamless debugging experience, allowing developers to edit and refactor code directly within the IDE and instantly see the effects of their changes on the application's behavior. Moreover, Delphi's version control integration facilitates collaboration and ensures that debugging changes are tracked and managed effectively throughout the development lifecycle.

bashCopy code

Example of editing code in Delphi IDE Ctrl + Shift + E

In summary, the debugging process in Delphi is a systematic and iterative approach to identifying, analyzing, diagnosing, and resolving issues in software applications. By leveraging Delphi's powerful debugging tools and integrated development environment, developers can streamline the debugging process and efficiently address issues, ensuring the reliability, functionality, and quality of their Delphi applications. From reproducing issues to analyzing runtime behavior, tracing execution paths, and implementing corrective actions, Delphi provides developers with the tools and capabilities they need to effectively debug their code and deliver robust, high-quality software solutions.

Chapter 2: Utilizing Delphi Debugger Tools

Exploring Delphi's built-in debugger is an essential aspect of mastering software development with Delphi, as it provides developers with powerful tools and capabilities for diagnosing and resolving issues in their applications. Delphi's debugger is seamlessly integrated into its integrated development environment (IDE), offering a comprehensive set of features and functionalities to streamline the debugging process and enhance developer productivity. One of the key features of Delphi's debugger is its support for breakpoints, which enable developers to pause the execution of their code at specific points and examine the program's state and behavior. By setting breakpoints at critical junctures in the code, developers can gain insights into the flow of control and identify potential issues or anomalies.

bashCopy code

Example of setting a breakpoint in Delphi IDE Ctrl + F5

Moreover, Delphi's debugger provides developers with the ability to inspect and modify variables, objects, and expressions in real-time, allowing them to track changes and diagnose issues as they occur. The debugger's watch list feature enables developers to monitor the values of selected variables and expressions during program execution, providing valuable insights into their behavior and facilitating the debugging process. Additionally, Delphi's debugger offers support for conditional breakpoints, which allow developers to specify conditions under which the breakpoint should be triggered, enabling them to focus their debugging efforts on specific scenarios or conditions.

bashCopy code

```
# Example of adding a watch expression in Delphi IDE
Alt + W
```

Furthermore, Delphi's debugger includes a call stack window, which provides developers with a visual representation of the sequence of function calls leading up to the current execution point. By examining the call stack, developers can trace the execution path of their code and identify potential points of failure or unexpected behavior. Additionally, the call stack window allows developers to navigate through the call hierarchy and inspect the state of variables and objects at different levels of the stack, facilitating the diagnosis of issues and the understanding of program flow.

bashCopy code

```
# Example of accessing the call stack in Delphi IDE Ctrl +
Alt + C
```

Another useful feature of Delphi's debugger is its support for debugging multi-threaded applications, which allows developers to debug code running in multiple threads simultaneously. Delphi's debugger provides tools for monitoring and controlling the execution of threads, including the ability to set breakpoints and step through code in individual threads, enabling developers to diagnose issues related to thread synchronization, race conditions, and concurrency. Additionally, Delphi's debugger offers support for debugging remote applications, allowing developers to debug code running on remote machines or devices from within the IDE.

bashCopy code

Example of debugging a multi-threaded application in Delphi IDE Ctrl + Alt + T

In summary, exploring Delphi's built-in debugger is essential for mastering software development with Delphi and ensuring the reliability, functionality, and quality of Delphi applications. With its comprehensive set of features and capabilities, including breakpoints, watch lists, call stack navigation, and support for multi-threaded and remote debugging, Delphi's debugger provides developers with powerful tools for diagnosing and resolving issues in their applications. By leveraging Delphi's debugger effectively, developers can streamline the debugging process, accelerate development workflows, and deliver robust, high-quality software solutions to their users.

Using debugger features for efficient debugging is essential for developers to identify and resolve issues in their code effectively, ensuring the reliability and quality of their software applications. Modern integrated development environments (IDEs), such as Delphi, provide a comprehensive set of debugger features and functionalities that streamline the debugging process and enhance developer productivity. One of the fundamental debugger features is breakpoints, which allow developers to pause the execution of their code at specific points and examine its state and behavior. By setting breakpoints strategically at critical junctures in the code, developers can gain insights into the flow of control and identify potential issues or anomalies.

bashCopy code

Example of setting a breakpoint in Delphi IDE F5

Additionally, debugger features such as watch lists enable developers to monitor the values of variables and expressions in real-time during program execution. By adding variables and expressions to the watch list, developers can track changes and diagnose issues as they occur, facilitating the debugging process. Moreover, watch lists provide developers with visibility into the state of their code, helping them identify unexpected behavior or discrepancies and make informed decisions about corrective actions.

bashCopy code

Example of adding a watch expression in Delphi IDE Ctrl + F4

Another useful debugger feature is the call stack window, which provides developers with a visual representation of the sequence of function calls leading up to the current execution point. By examining the call stack, developers can trace the execution path of their code and identify potential points of failure or unexpected behavior. Additionally, the call stack window allows developers to navigate through the call hierarchy and inspect the state of variables and objects at different levels of the stack, facilitating the diagnosis of issues and the understanding of program flow.

bashCopy code

Example of accessing the call stack in Delphi IDE Ctrl + Alt + C

Conditional breakpoints are another powerful debugger feature that enables developers to specify conditions under which a breakpoint should be triggered. By setting conditions based on variable values, expressions, or program state, developers can focus their debugging efforts on specific scenarios or conditions, reducing the time and effort required to identify and diagnose issues. Conditional breakpoints help developers narrow down the scope of their debugging sessions and target specific areas of concern, leading to more efficient debugging workflows and faster issue resolution.

bashCopy code

Example of setting a conditional breakpoint in Delphi IDE Shift + F5

Furthermore, debugger features such as step-by-step execution and variable inspection enable developers to control the flow of their code and examine its state at each step of execution. By stepping through code line by line and inspecting the values of variables and objects, developers can gain a deeper understanding of their code's behavior and identify issues more effectively. Moreover, Delphi's debugger offers support for debugging multi-threaded applications, allowing developers to debug code running in multiple threads simultaneously.

bashCopy code

Example of stepping through code in Delphi IDE F7 (Step Over) F8 (Step Into) Shift + F7 (Run to Cursor)

In summary, leveraging debugger features for efficient debugging is crucial for developers to identify and resolve issues in their code effectively. By using features such as breakpoints, watch lists, call stacks, conditional breakpoints, and step-by-step execution, developers can streamline the debugging process, accelerate issue resolution, and deliver high-quality software applications to their users. By mastering debugger features and incorporating them into their development workflows, developers can enhance their productivity and ensure the reliability and quality of their software products.

Chapter 3: Understanding Common Programming Errors

Identifying and resolving syntax errors is a fundamental aspect of software development, essential for ensuring the correctness and functionality of code. Syntax errors occur when code does not conform to the rules and conventions of the programming language, leading to compilation or runtime errors. Detecting and fixing syntax errors is critical for developers to maintain the integrity of their codebase and prevent issues from proliferating throughout the application. One common type of syntax error is a missing semicolon at the end of a statement, which can cause compilation errors and prevent the code from being executed properly.

bashCopy code

```
# Example of identifying and fixing a missing semicolon
in Delphi IDE Shift + Ctrl + C
```

Another common syntax error is misspelling or incorrectly referencing variables, functions, or keywords, leading to compilation errors or unexpected behavior in the code. By carefully reviewing the code and ensuring that all identifiers are spelled correctly and properly referenced, developers can prevent syntax errors and maintain code integrity. Additionally, Delphi's integrated development environment (IDE) provides features such as code completion and syntax highlighting, which help developers identify and correct syntax errors in real-time.

```
bashCopy code
```
Example of using code completion in Delphi IDE Ctrl + Space

Furthermore, mismatched parentheses, brackets, or braces are a common source of syntax errors in code, causing compilation errors or unexpected behavior. By carefully matching opening and closing symbols and ensuring that they are properly nested, developers can prevent syntax errors and maintain code readability and consistency. Delphi's IDE provides features such as bracket matching and indentation guides, which help developers visualize the structure of their code and identify mismatched symbols.

```
bashCopy code
```
Example of matching brackets in Delphi IDE Ctrl + [

Additionally, Delphi's compiler provides detailed error messages and diagnostics, which help developers pinpoint the location and nature of syntax errors in their code. By carefully reviewing compiler output and error messages, developers can identify syntax errors and take corrective actions to resolve them effectively. Moreover, Delphi's IDE offers features such as code navigation and error highlighting, which help developers quickly locate syntax errors and navigate to their respective locations in the codebase.

```
bashCopy code
```
Example of navigating to an error location in Delphi IDE F8 (Go to Next Error) Shift + F8 (Go to Previous Error)

In summary, identifying and resolving syntax errors is a critical skill for software developers, essential for maintaining the integrity and functionality of code. By carefully reviewing code, using IDE features such as code completion and syntax highlighting, and leveraging compiler diagnostics, developers can effectively detect and fix syntax errors in their codebase. By mastering syntax error identification and resolution techniques, developers can improve code quality, prevent issues, and deliver reliable and robust software applications to end-users.

Handling runtime errors in Delphi programs is an essential aspect of software development, crucial for ensuring the stability and reliability of applications. Runtime errors occur during the execution of a program and can lead to unexpected behavior, crashes, or even data corruption if not handled properly. Identifying and addressing runtime errors effectively is critical for developers to maintain the integrity of their codebase and provide a seamless user experience. One common type of runtime error in Delphi programs is the access violation error, which occurs when a program attempts to access memory that it does not have permission to access.

bashCopy code
Example of handling access violation errors in Delphi IDE Ctrl + Shift + E

Another common runtime error is the division by zero error, which occurs when a program attempts to divide a number by zero, leading to undefined behavior and potential program crashes. To prevent division by zero errors, developers can use conditional statements or exception handling mechanisms to check for zero denominators and handle them gracefully. Delphi's integrated development environment (IDE) provides features such as code analysis and debugging tools, which help developers identify and diagnose runtime errors in their codebase.

bashCopy code

Example of using exception handling in Delphi IDE try // Code that may raise an exception except // Handle the exception end;

Additionally, Delphi's runtime environment provides built-in exception classes and error handling mechanisms, allowing developers to catch and handle exceptions gracefully. By using exception handling constructs such as try-except blocks or try-finally blocks, developers can intercept and handle runtime errors at runtime, preventing them from propagating and crashing the application. Moreover, Delphi's IDE offers features such as exception breakpoints and exception tracing, which help developers pinpoint the location and nature of runtime errors in their codebase.

bashCopy code

Example of setting an exception breakpoint in Delphi IDE Ctrl + Shift + B

Furthermore, Delphi's runtime library provides functions and procedures for retrieving detailed error information and diagnostics, enabling developers to diagnose and troubleshoot runtime errors effectively.

By leveraging runtime error reporting mechanisms and logging frameworks, developers can capture and log runtime errors to facilitate debugging and analysis. Moreover, Delphi's IDE offers features such as runtime error logging and error reporting tools, which help developers track and analyze runtime errors in their applications.

bashCopy code

Example of logging runtime errors in Delphi IDE try // Code that may raise an exception except on E: Exception do // Log the exception end;

In summary, handling runtime errors in Delphi programs is crucial for ensuring the stability and reliability of applications. By using exception handling mechanisms, debugging tools, and error reporting features provided by Delphi's IDE and runtime environment, developers can effectively identify, diagnose, and resolve runtime errors in their codebase. By mastering runtime error handling techniques and incorporating them into their development workflows, developers can deliver robust, high-quality software applications that meet the needs and expectations of end-users.

Chapter 4: Breakpoints and Stepping Through Code

Setting and managing breakpoints is a fundamental aspect of debugging in software development, crucial for identifying and diagnosing issues in code effectively. Breakpoints are markers that developers can place in their code to pause execution at specific points, allowing them to inspect the program state, variables, and execution flow. By strategically setting breakpoints at critical junctures in the code, developers can isolate problematic areas and gain insights into the behavior of their applications. One common way to set a breakpoint in Delphi IDE is by clicking on the left margin of the code editor window, next to the line number where you want to pause execution.

bashCopy code

Example of setting a breakpoint in Delphi IDE F5

Once breakpoints are set, developers can manage them using various techniques and tools provided by Delphi's IDE. For instance, developers can enable or disable breakpoints individually or all at once to control when the program pauses execution. Additionally, developers can set conditional breakpoints, which only pause execution when specific conditions are met, such as when a variable reaches a certain value. This allows developers to focus their debugging efforts on specific scenarios or conditions, improving efficiency and productivity.

bashCopy code

```
# Example of setting a conditional breakpoint in Delphi
IDE Shift + F5
```

Moreover, Delphi's IDE offers features such as breakpoint lists and breakpoint windows, which provide developers with visibility into all set breakpoints and allow them to manage them conveniently. By reviewing the breakpoint list, developers can quickly identify the locations of all set breakpoints in their codebase and make adjustments as needed. Furthermore, Delphi's IDE provides options for logging breakpoints, allowing developers to log messages or perform custom actions when breakpoints are hit, enhancing the debugging experience.

bashCopy code

```
# Example of accessing the breakpoint list in Delphi IDE
Ctrl + Alt + B
```

Additionally, Delphi's debugger provides advanced breakpoint features, such as hit count breakpoints, which allow developers to specify the number of times a breakpoint must be hit before pausing execution. This feature is useful for debugging loops or repetitive code segments, where developers may only want to pause execution after a certain number of iterations. By using hit count breakpoints, developers can streamline the debugging process and focus their efforts on specific iterations or occurrences of code execution.

bashCopy code

```
# Example of setting a hit count breakpoint in Delphi
IDE Ctrl + Shift + B
```

Furthermore, Delphi's debugger offers options for breakpoint actions, allowing developers to specify actions to be performed when breakpoints are hit, such as logging messages, evaluating expressions, or modifying variable values. By defining breakpoint actions, developers can automate repetitive debugging tasks and streamline their workflow, improving efficiency and productivity. Additionally, Delphi's debugger provides features such as breakpoint conditions and expressions, which allow developers to specify conditions or expressions that must be true for a breakpoint to be hit, providing greater flexibility and control over the debugging process.

bashCopy code

```
# Example of setting a breakpoint action in Delphi IDE
Ctrl + Shift + E
```

In summary, setting and managing breakpoints is a crucial aspect of debugging in software development, essential for identifying and diagnosing issues effectively. By strategically setting breakpoints, enabling conditional breakpoints, and leveraging advanced breakpoint features provided by Delphi's IDE, developers can streamline the debugging process, improve productivity, and deliver high-quality software applications to end-users. By mastering breakpoint management techniques and incorporating them into their development workflows, developers can enhance their debugging skills and become more proficient in identifying and resolving issues in their codebase.

Navigating code execution with step commands is a fundamental aspect of the debugging process in software development, allowing developers to trace the flow of execution through their code and identify issues effectively. Step commands enable developers to execute code one instruction at a time, allowing them to observe changes in variables, inspect program state, and identify the root causes of bugs. In Delphi's integrated development environment (IDE), developers can navigate code execution using step commands such as Step Over, Step Into, and Step Out.

bashCopy code

```
# Example of stepping over a line of code in Delphi IDE
F7
```

Step Over is a commonly used command that allows developers to execute the current line of code and move to the next line without stepping into function or method calls. This command is useful for quickly traversing through code segments and observing changes in variables without diving into the details of function implementations. By using Step Over strategically, developers can maintain focus on the high-level logic of their code and identify potential issues efficiently.

bashCopy code

```
# Example of stepping into a function or method call in
Delphi IDE F8
```

On the other hand, Step Into allows developers to delve deeper into the details of code execution by stepping into function or method calls. When developers encounter a function or method call while debugging, they can use Step Into to enter the called function or method and execute its instructions one by one. This command is valuable for understanding the inner workings of functions or methods and diagnosing issues that may occur within them. By using Step Into, developers can trace the flow of execution through nested function calls and pinpoint the locations of bugs more accurately.

bashCopy code

Example of stepping out of a function or method call in Delphi IDE Shift + F8

Moreover, Step Out enables developers to exit the current function or method and return to the calling code context. When developers find themselves inside a function or method while debugging and wish to return to the caller, they can use Step Out to execute the remaining instructions of the current function or method and return to the calling code context. This command is beneficial for quickly navigating out of nested function calls and resuming code execution at the appropriate level of abstraction.

bashCopy code

Example of restarting the debugging process in Delphi IDE Ctrl + F2

Furthermore, Delphi's IDE provides features such as restart debugging, which allows developers to restart the debugging process from the beginning of the application execution. This feature is useful for resetting the debugging environment and re-executing the application from the initial state, providing developers with a clean slate to diagnose issues and test fixes. By utilizing restart debugging, developers can streamline their debugging workflow and ensure thorough testing of their applications.

```bash
# Example of toggling breakpoints in Delphi IDE F5
```

Additionally, developers can toggle breakpoints during debugging sessions to control the flow of execution and pause execution at specific points in the code. By strategically placing breakpoints at critical junctures in the code, developers can observe the program state, inspect variables, and diagnose issues effectively. Delphi's IDE provides features such as breakpoint lists and breakpoint windows, which allow developers to manage breakpoints conveniently and gain visibility into all set breakpoints in their codebase.

In summary, navigating code execution with step commands is a crucial skill for developers, essential for debugging and diagnosing issues in software applications. By mastering step commands such as Step Over, Step Into, and Step Out, developers can trace the flow of execution through their code, identify bugs efficiently, and deliver high-quality software applications to end-users. By incorporating step commands into their debugging workflow and leveraging advanced debugging features provided by Delphi's IDE, developers can streamline the debugging process, improve productivity, and ensure the reliability and stability of their codebase.

Chapter 5: Inspecting Variables and Memory

Viewing and modifying variable values is a crucial aspect of debugging and troubleshooting in software development, allowing developers to inspect the state of variables at specific points in their code and make necessary adjustments to resolve issues effectively. In Delphi's integrated development environment (IDE), developers can access and manipulate variable values using various techniques and tools provided by the debugger. One common way to view variable values in Delphi IDE is by using the Watches window, which displays the values of specified variables in real-time during debugging sessions.

bashCopy code

Example of opening the Watches window in Delphi IDE Ctrl + Alt + W

The Watches window provides developers with a convenient interface to monitor the values of variables as they step through their code during debugging sessions. By adding variables of interest to the Watches window, developers can track changes in their values and detect anomalies or unexpected behavior. Additionally, developers can modify variable values directly from the Watches window, allowing them to test hypotheses and experiment with different scenarios to diagnose issues accurately.

bashCopy code

Example of modifying a variable value in Delphi IDE's Watches window DoubleClick on the value field of the variable

Moreover, Delphi's debugger offers features such as breakpoints with expressions, which allow developers to set breakpoints based on specific conditions or expressions involving variables. By using breakpoints with expressions, developers can pause execution at critical points in their code and evaluate the values of variables in the context of conditional statements or expressions, providing greater insight into the behavior of their applications.

bashCopy code

Example of setting a breakpoint with an expression in Delphi IDE Right-click on the breakpoint line -> Breakpoint properties -> Condition tab

Furthermore, Delphi's IDE provides tools for inspecting variable values during runtime, such as the Evaluate/Modify window, which allows developers to evaluate expressions and modify variable values interactively. By entering expressions into the Evaluate/Modify window, developers can calculate values based on existing variables and perform operations to analyze the behavior of their code dynamically.

bashCopy code

Example of opening the Evaluate/Modify window in Delphi IDE Ctrl + F7

Additionally, Delphi's debugger offers features such as conditional breakpoints, which allow developers to set breakpoints that only pause execution when specific conditions are met. By specifying conditions based on variable values or expressions, developers can focus their debugging efforts on specific scenarios or conditions, improving efficiency and productivity.

bashCopy code

```
# Example of setting a conditional breakpoint in Delphi
IDE Right-click on the breakpoint line -> Breakpoint
properties -> Condition tab
```

Moreover, Delphi's IDE provides options for logging variable values during debugging sessions, allowing developers to log messages or values of variables to a log file for later analysis. By enabling logging for specific variables, developers can capture important information about the state of their applications and diagnose issues more effectively.

bashCopy code

```
# Example of enabling logging for a variable in Delphi
IDE Right-click on the variable -> Log variable value
```

In summary, viewing and modifying variable values is a crucial aspect of debugging and troubleshooting in software development, essential for diagnosing issues and resolving them effectively. By leveraging features such as the Watches window, breakpoints with expressions, the Evaluate/Modify window, conditional breakpoints, and logging variable values provided by Delphi's IDE, developers can gain greater insight into the behavior of their applications and ensure the reliability and stability of their codebase. By incorporating variable inspection and manipulation techniques into their debugging workflow, developers can streamline the debugging process, improve productivity, and deliver high-quality software applications to end-users.

Examining memory usage during debugging sessions is a crucial aspect of software development, allowing developers to monitor the allocation and deallocation of memory resources in their applications and identify potential memory-related issues such as leaks or excessive consumption. In Delphi's integrated development environment (IDE), developers can analyze memory usage using various tools and techniques provided by the debugger. One common approach is to utilize the Memory view window, which displays the contents of memory at specific addresses and allows developers to inspect the values stored in memory during debugging sessions.

bashCopy code

```
# Example of opening the Memory view window in
Delphi IDE Alt + Ctrl + M
```

The Memory view window provides developers with a low-level view of the memory layout of their applications, allowing them to examine the values stored in memory locations and identify patterns or anomalies that may indicate memory-related issues. By navigating through memory addresses and inspecting the values stored at those locations, developers can gain insight into the memory usage patterns of their applications and detect potential issues such as buffer overflows or uninitialized memory accesses.

bashCopy code

```
# Example of navigating memory addresses in the
Memory view window Enter memory address in the
address field
```

Moreover, Delphi's debugger offers features such as
memory breakpoints, which allow developers to set
breakpoints based on memory access events such as
read, write, or execute operations on specific memory
addresses. By using memory breakpoints, developers
can pause execution when certain memory locations are
accessed, allowing them to track memory usage
patterns and identify potential issues related to
memory access violations or incorrect memory
accesses.

bashCopy code

```
# Example of setting a memory breakpoint in Delphi IDE
Right-click on the memory address -> Breakpoint
properties -> Set memory breakpoint
```

Additionally, Delphi's IDE provides tools for analyzing
memory usage over time, such as the Memory Usage
view, which displays a graphical representation of
memory usage trends during debugging sessions. By
monitoring memory usage trends over time, developers
can identify memory leaks or excessive memory
consumption patterns and take corrective actions to
optimize memory usage and improve application
performance.

bashCopy code

```
# Example of opening the Memory Usage view in Delphi
IDE View -> Debug Windows -> Memory Usage
```

Furthermore, Delphi's debugger offers features such as memory allocation tracking, which allows developers to track memory allocations and deallocations in their applications during debugging sessions. By enabling memory allocation tracking, developers can identify memory leaks or inefficient memory allocation patterns and optimize memory usage to ensure efficient utilization of resources.

```bash
# Example of enabling memory allocation tracking in
Delphi IDE Debug -> Enable Memory Usage Tracker
```

Moreover, Delphi's IDE provides options for profiling memory usage during debugging sessions, allowing developers to analyze memory allocation and deallocation patterns and identify areas of improvement. By profiling memory usage, developers can identify memory-intensive operations or data structures and optimize them to reduce memory consumption and improve application performance.

```bash
# Example of profiling memory usage in Delphi IDE
Debug -> Profile Memory Usage
```

In summary, examining memory usage during debugging sessions is essential for identifying and resolving memory-related issues in software applications. By leveraging tools and techniques such as the Memory view window, memory breakpoints, memory usage tracking, and memory profiling provided by Delphi's IDE, developers can gain insight into the memory usage patterns of their applications and optimize memory usage to ensure efficient resource utilization and improve application performance. By incorporating memory usage analysis into their debugging workflow, developers can deliver high-quality software applications that meet performance and reliability standards.

Chapter 6: Advanced Debugging Techniques for Multithreaded Applications

Debugging multithreaded applications poses unique challenges for developers due to the concurrent execution of multiple threads, which can lead to race conditions, deadlocks, and other synchronization issues that are difficult to diagnose and reproduce. In Delphi's integrated development environment (IDE), developers can use various tools and techniques to tackle these challenges and effectively debug multithreaded applications. One common approach is to utilize the Threads window, which provides developers with a comprehensive view of all active threads in their application and allows them to inspect each thread's call stack, state, and associated resources.

bashCopy code
Example of opening the Threads window in Delphi IDE
Ctrl + Alt + T

The Threads window enables developers to monitor the execution of multiple threads simultaneously, making it easier to identify synchronization issues and thread-related anomalies. By examining the call stacks of individual threads, developers can pinpoint the locations in their code where threads are interacting and identify potential points of contention or race conditions.

bashCopy code

```
# Example of inspecting the call stack of a thread in
Delphi IDE's Threads window Select the thread of
interest -> View Call Stack
```

Moreover, Delphi's debugger offers features such as breakpoints with thread conditions, which allow developers to set breakpoints that only trigger when specific threads reach certain conditions or states. By using breakpoints with thread conditions, developers can focus their debugging efforts on specific threads or scenarios, making it easier to isolate and diagnose multithreading issues.

bashCopy code

```
# Example of setting a breakpoint with a thread
condition in Delphi IDE Right-click on the breakpoint
line -> Breakpoint properties -> Thread tab
```

Additionally, Delphi's IDE provides tools for analyzing thread synchronization primitives, such as mutexes, semaphores, and critical sections, which are commonly used to coordinate access to shared resources in multithreaded applications. By inspecting the state of synchronization primitives during debugging sessions, developers can identify instances of improper synchronization or deadlock conditions and take corrective actions to resolve them.

bashCopy code

```
# Example of inspecting synchronization primitives in
Delphi IDE Debug -> Analyze Synchronization Primitives
```

Furthermore, Delphi's debugger offers features such as thread profiling, which allows developers to analyze the behavior and performance of individual threads during runtime. By profiling thread activity, developers can identify threads that are consuming excessive CPU time or experiencing long execution times, indicating potential performance bottlenecks or inefficiencies in thread scheduling.

bashCopy code

Example of profiling thread activity in Delphi IDE Debug -> Profile Threads

Moreover, Delphi's IDE provides options for debugging multithreaded applications remotely, allowing developers to debug applications running on remote machines or target platforms. By connecting to a remote debugging session, developers can analyze the behavior of multithreaded applications in real-world environments and diagnose issues that may not be reproducible in local development environments.

bashCopy code

Example of initiating a remote debugging session in Delphi IDE Debug -> Attach to Process (Remote Debugging)

In summary, debugging multithreaded applications presents unique challenges for developers, but with the right tools and techniques provided by Delphi's IDE, developers can effectively tackle these challenges and ensure the reliability and performance of their multithreaded applications. By leveraging features such as the Threads window, breakpoints with thread conditions, synchronization primitive analysis, thread profiling, and remote debugging support, developers can identify and resolve multithreading issues efficiently, leading to the delivery of robust and high-performance software applications.

Debugging race conditions and deadlocks is an intricate task for software developers, especially in concurrent programming environments where multiple threads contend for shared resources. These issues can lead to unpredictable behavior, application crashes, or system hangs, making them critical to address. In Delphi's integrated development environment (IDE), developers can employ various strategies and tools to identify and resolve race conditions and deadlocks effectively. One key approach is to use synchronization primitives such as mutexes, semaphores, and critical sections to coordinate access to shared resources and prevent concurrent access conflicts.

```bash
bashCopy code
# Example of using synchronization primitives in Delphi
IDE TMonitor.Enter(myObject); try // Critical section
code finally TMonitor.Exit(myObject); end;
```

By encapsulating critical sections of code within synchronization primitives, developers can enforce mutual exclusion and ensure that only one thread accesses a shared resource at a time, thereby mitigating the risk of race conditions. Additionally, Delphi's debugger provides features such as breakpoint conditions and watch expressions, which allow developers to monitor variables and conditions that may contribute to race conditions or deadlocks.

bashCopy code

Example of setting a breakpoint condition in Delphi IDE Right-click on the breakpoint line -> Breakpoint properties -> Condition tab

With breakpoint conditions, developers can halt program execution when specific conditions related to race conditions or deadlocks are met, enabling them to inspect the program state and identify potential issues. Moreover, Delphi's IDE offers tools for analyzing thread activity and synchronization behavior, such as the Threads window and the Analyze Synchronization Primitives feature.

bashCopy code

Example of analyzing synchronization primitives in Delphi IDE Debug -> Analyze Synchronization Primitives

By examining the state of synchronization primitives and thread activity during debugging sessions, developers can gain insight into the interactions between threads and identify potential causes of race conditions or deadlocks. Furthermore, Delphi's IDE provides options for simulating and reproducing race conditions and deadlocks in controlled environments, allowing developers to debug these issues more effectively.

bashCopy code

Example of simulating race conditions in Delphi IDE Debug -> Simulate Race Condition

By simulating race conditions and deadlocks, developers can observe the behavior of their applications under different scenarios and identify potential weaknesses or vulnerabilities. Additionally, Delphi's debugger offers features such as memory profiling and performance monitoring, which allow developers to analyze memory usage and resource consumption patterns during debugging sessions.

bashCopy code

```
# Example of profiling memory usage in Delphi IDE
Debug -> Profile Memory Usage
```

By profiling memory usage and performance metrics, developers can identify inefficiencies or resource bottlenecks that may contribute to race conditions or deadlocks. In summary, debugging race conditions and deadlocks requires a systematic approach and the use of appropriate tools and techniques. With Delphi's IDE, developers can leverage features such as synchronization primitives, breakpoint conditions, thread analysis tools, and simulation capabilities to identify and resolve these challenging issues effectively, ensuring the reliability and stability of their software applications.

Chapter 7: Debugging Techniques for GUI Applications

Debugging user interface (UI) issues is an essential aspect of software development, particularly in applications where the user experience plays a critical role. These issues can manifest in various forms, such as layout inconsistencies, unresponsive controls, or unexpected behavior in UI elements. In Delphi's integrated development environment (IDE), developers have access to a range of tools and techniques to diagnose and resolve UI-related bugs efficiently. One common approach is to utilize the LiveBindings feature, which allows developers to establish data bindings between UI controls and data sources, enabling real-time updates and synchronization between the two.

bashCopy code

Example of using LiveBindings in Delphi IDE Right-click on a UI control -> Bind Visually

By visually binding UI controls to data sources, developers can ensure that changes in data reflect immediately in the UI, facilitating the identification of any discrepancies or anomalies. Additionally, Delphi's IDE provides tools for inspecting and manipulating UI controls at runtime, such as the Object Inspector and the Component Tree view.

bashCopy code

Example of accessing the Object Inspector in Delphi IDE View -> Object Inspector

Through the Object Inspector, developers can examine the properties and event handlers of UI controls, allowing them to identify potential misconfigurations or inconsistencies that may contribute to UI issues. Moreover, Delphi's debugger offers features such as visual form inheritance and runtime form manipulation, which enable developers to analyze and modify UI layouts dynamically during debugging sessions.

bashCopy code

```
# Example of using visual form inheritance in Delphi IDE
Right-click on a form file -> Inherit Form
```

By leveraging visual form inheritance, developers can inspect the hierarchy of UI elements and identify any issues related to layout inheritance or composition. Furthermore, Delphi's IDE provides options for simulating user interactions and UI events, allowing developers to test the responsiveness and behavior of UI controls under different scenarios.

bashCopy code

```
# Example of simulating UI events in Delphi IDE Debug -> Simulate User Interaction
```

By simulating user interactions, developers can identify potential edge cases or corner scenarios that may lead to unexpected UI behavior or inconsistencies. Additionally, Delphi's debugger offers features such as UI inspection tools and accessibility testing capabilities, which enable developers to assess the accessibility and usability of their UI designs.

bashCopy code

Example of accessing accessibility testing tools in Delphi IDE Debug -> Accessibility Testing

By evaluating the accessibility and usability of UI designs, developers can ensure that their applications cater to a diverse range of users and comply with accessibility standards. In summary, debugging UI issues requires a combination of tools, techniques, and best practices to identify and resolve potential issues effectively. With Delphi's IDE, developers can leverage features such as LiveBindings, visual form inheritance, runtime form manipulation, and accessibility testing to diagnose and address UI-related bugs efficiently, ultimately delivering a seamless and intuitive user experience.

Identifying and fixing common GUI bugs is a fundamental aspect of software development, particularly in applications where the graphical user interface (GUI) plays a significant role in user interaction. GUI bugs can encompass a wide range of issues, from layout inconsistencies and alignment problems to unresponsive or malfunctioning controls. In Delphi's integrated development environment (IDE), developers have access to various tools and techniques to diagnose and resolve these bugs efficiently. One common GUI bug is the misalignment of UI elements, which can occur due to incorrect positioning or sizing properties.

bashCopy code

```
# Example of adjusting UI element positioning in Delphi
IDE Right-click on the UI element -> Position -> Align to
Grid
```

By aligning UI elements to a grid, developers can ensure consistent spacing and alignment, helping to eliminate misalignment issues. Another common GUI bug is the overlapping of controls, which can occur when controls are positioned too closely together or when their bounding boxes intersect.

bashCopy code
```
# Example of adjusting control positioning in Delphi IDE
Right-click on the overlapping control -> Bring to Front
```

By adjusting the z-order of controls, developers can ensure that overlapping controls are correctly layered, preventing visual clutter and ensuring proper interaction. Additionally, GUI bugs can manifest as unresponsive or non-functional controls, which may occur due to event handling errors or incorrect control properties.

bashCopy code
```
# Example of debugging event handling in Delphi IDE
Set breakpoints in event handlers -> Debug -> Run
```

By debugging event handlers and inspecting control properties, developers can identify potential issues that may cause controls to become unresponsive or malfunction. Furthermore, GUI bugs can include graphical artifacts or rendering glitches, which may arise due to issues with graphics rendering or GPU acceleration.

bashCopy code

Example of adjusting graphics rendering settings in Delphi IDE Project Options -> Application -> Enable GPU acceleration

By adjusting graphics rendering settings and disabling GPU acceleration if necessary, developers can mitigate rendering glitches and ensure a smooth graphical experience for users. Moreover, GUI bugs may involve incorrect data binding or synchronization between UI controls and underlying data sources.

bashCopy code

Example of troubleshooting data binding issues in Delphi IDE Inspect data bindings in Object Inspector -> Debug -> Evaluate/Modify

By inspecting data bindings and evaluating data synchronization during runtime, developers can identify discrepancies between UI controls and data sources, allowing them to correct any data binding issues effectively. Additionally, GUI bugs can arise from platform-specific differences or inconsistencies in UI behavior across different operating systems or screen resolutions.

bashCopy code

Example of testing UI behavior on different platforms in Delphi IDE Deploy application to target platforms -> Test on different devices/OS versions

By testing UI behavior on various platforms and devices, developers can identify platform-specific GUI bugs and ensure consistent user experiences across different environments. In summary, identifying and fixing common GUI bugs requires a systematic approach and the use of appropriate tools and techniques. With Delphi's IDE, developers can leverage features such as alignment tools, z-order manipulation, event debugging, graphics rendering settings, data binding inspection, and platform testing to diagnose and resolve GUI-related issues efficiently, ultimately delivering a polished and user-friendly application.

Chapter 8: Remote Debugging and Error Reporting

Debugging applications running on remote machines is a crucial aspect of software development, particularly in distributed or client-server environments where applications may be deployed across multiple servers or devices. This process involves diagnosing and resolving bugs or issues in the code remotely, without direct access to the development environment. In scenarios where the application runs on a remote machine, accessing the debugging tools and logs typically requires remote debugging techniques, which can be facilitated using various tools and methodologies. One common approach is to use remote debugging features provided by integrated development environments such as Visual Studio or Delphi. These IDEs offer built-in support for remote debugging, allowing developers to connect to remote instances of their applications and debug them as if they were running locally.

bashCopy code

Example of starting remote debugging session in Visual Studio Open project in Visual Studio -> Debug -> Attach to Process

By attaching to the process running on the remote machine, developers can set breakpoints, inspect variables, and step through the code to identify and resolve issues. Similarly, in Delphi's IDE, developers can utilize remote debugging capabilities to connect to a remote instance of their application and debug it remotely.

bashCopy code

Example of remote debugging in Delphi IDE Open project in Delphi IDE -> Run -> Remote Debugging

Through remote debugging in Delphi, developers can debug applications running on remote machines, inspecting runtime behavior and diagnosing issues effectively. Additionally, remote debugging can be facilitated using command-line tools and utilities, which allow developers to debug applications remotely without relying on a graphical interface. For example, the gdb (GNU Debugger) command-line tool is commonly used for remote debugging in C/C++ applications.

bashCopy code

Example of remote debugging with gdb gdb <executable> --tui

By connecting to the remote machine via SSH and launching the gdb debugger with the target executable, developers can debug the application remotely, inspecting memory, setting breakpoints, and stepping through the code as needed. Moreover, remote debugging can be complemented with logging and tracing mechanisms, which allow developers to capture and analyze runtime information and events remotely. By incorporating logging statements strategically into the code, developers can generate detailed logs that provide insights into the application's behavior and execution flow.

bashCopy code

```
# Example of enabling logging in Java application
logger.info("Debugging information");
```

By logging debugging information to a file or a centralized logging server, developers can monitor the application's behavior remotely and identify any anomalies or issues. Furthermore, remote debugging can be integrated with continuous integration (CI) and continuous deployment (CD) pipelines, allowing developers to debug applications automatically as part of the deployment process.

bashCopy code

```
# Example of remote debugging in CI/CD pipeline Set
up remote debugging as a step in CI/CD pipeline
configuration
```

By incorporating remote debugging into CI/CD pipelines, developers can ensure that applications are thoroughly tested and debugged before deployment, minimizing the risk of introducing bugs or issues into production environments. In summary, debugging applications running on remote machines requires a combination of tools, techniques, and best practices to diagnose and resolve issues effectively. Whether through integrated development environments, command-line tools, logging mechanisms, or CI/CD pipelines, developers have various options for remote debugging, allowing them to ensure the reliability and stability of their applications in distributed environments.

Implementing error reporting mechanisms in Delphi

programs is a critical aspect of software development aimed at enhancing application reliability and facilitating efficient debugging processes. Error reporting mechanisms enable developers to capture and analyze runtime errors, exceptions, and unexpected behaviors, providing valuable insights into the application's stability and performance. In Delphi, developers can implement error reporting mechanisms using various techniques, including logging frameworks, exception handling, and external error reporting services. One common approach is to integrate a logging framework into the Delphi application, which allows developers to record important events, errors, and diagnostic information during runtime.

bashCopy code

```
# Example of configuring logging in a Delphi application
Add logging library to project dependencies ->
Configure logging settings
```

By integrating a logging framework such as Log4Delphi or DLogger into the Delphi application, developers can log error messages, stack traces, and other relevant information to a file or a centralized logging server, facilitating error analysis and troubleshooting. Another approach to implementing error reporting mechanisms in Delphi programs is through robust exception handling strategies. Delphi provides built-in support for structured exception handling (SEH), allowing developers to catch and handle exceptions gracefully.

bashCopy code

Example of structured exception handling in Delphi try // Code that may throw exceptions except on E: Exception do // Handle the exception end;

By enclosing critical sections of code within try-except blocks, developers can intercept exceptions, log error details, and perform cleanup operations as needed, preventing application crashes and ensuring a smoother user experience. Additionally, Delphi applications can leverage external error reporting services to streamline the error reporting process and centralize error data collection and analysis.

bashCopy code

Example of integrating an external error reporting service in a Delphi application Configure error reporting service API integration -> Send error reports on exception

By integrating with error reporting services such as Sentry or Bugsnag, developers can automatically capture and report errors, exceptions, and crashes to a centralized dashboard, providing real-time visibility into application issues and facilitating proactive bug resolution. Moreover, Delphi applications can utilize structured logging techniques to enhance error reporting capabilities further.

bashCopy code

Example of structured logging in Delphi application Log.Error('An error occurred: ' + E.Message);

By incorporating structured logging statements into the codebase, developers can capture contextual information along with error messages, enabling more accurate diagnosis and resolution of application issues. Furthermore, Delphi programs can implement custom error reporting dialogs or screens to notify users of errors and guide them through the troubleshooting process.

bashCopy code

```
# Example of displaying a custom error reporting dialog in Delphi application ShowMessage('An unexpected error has occurred. Please contact support for assistance.');
```

By presenting users with informative error messages and guidance on how to proceed, developers can improve the user experience and facilitate timely resolution of application issues. Additionally, Delphi applications can utilize remote error reporting mechanisms to report errors and exceptions occurring in deployed instances back to the development team.

bashCopy code

```
# Example of remote error reporting configuration in Delphi application Set up error reporting endpoint -> Send error reports over HTTP(S)
```

By configuring the application to send error reports to a remote server or endpoint, developers can collect valuable diagnostic data from deployed instances, enabling them to identify and address issues in real-time. In summary, implementing error reporting mechanisms in Delphi programs is essential for maintaining application reliability, diagnosing issues effectively, and delivering a seamless user experience. By leveraging logging frameworks, exception handling strategies, external error reporting services, structured logging techniques, custom error reporting dialogs, and remote error reporting mechanisms, developers can enhance error detection, analysis, and resolution capabilities, ultimately ensuring the robustness and stability of their Delphi applications.

Chapter 9: Performance Profiling and Optimization

Profiling Delphi applications for performance bottlenecks is an indispensable practice in software development aimed at identifying and resolving performance issues that may degrade application responsiveness and efficiency. By analyzing various aspects of application execution, such as CPU usage, memory allocation, and I/O operations, developers can pinpoint bottlenecks and optimize critical sections of code to enhance overall performance. In Delphi, developers can leverage built-in profiling tools and third-party utilities to conduct comprehensive performance analysis and profiling.

One of the fundamental techniques for profiling Delphi applications is utilizing the built-in performance monitoring and profiling features provided by the Delphi IDE itself. With the Performance Analyzer tool, developers can collect and analyze performance data during application execution, allowing them to identify performance bottlenecks and hotspots in the code. The Performance Analyzer provides insights into CPU usage, memory consumption, function call timings, and other performance metrics, enabling developers to optimize critical code paths efficiently.

bashCopy code

```
# Example of using the Performance Analyzer in Delphi
IDE Navigate to Tools -> Performance Analyzer -> Start
Profiling
```

By initiating the Performance Analyzer within the Delphi IDE, developers can profile their applications in real-time or capture performance data for later analysis. The Performance Analyzer presents performance metrics in a visual manner, allowing developers to identify areas of concern and drill down into specific functions or modules causing performance degradation.

Another essential technique for profiling Delphi applications is leveraging third-party profiling tools and libraries, such as AQTime or ANTS Performance Profiler. These tools offer advanced profiling capabilities, including code instrumentation, call stack analysis, and memory profiling, allowing developers to conduct in-depth performance analysis and identify optimization opportunities.

bashCopy code

```
# Example of using AQTime for profiling Delphi applications Load the Delphi project into AQTime -> Configure profiling settings -> Start profiling
```

By integrating third-party profiling tools into the Delphi development workflow, developers can gain deeper insights into application performance and streamline the optimization process. These tools offer features such as code coverage analysis, performance comparisons, and profiling sessions management, enabling developers to track performance improvements over time and validate optimization efforts effectively.

Additionally, Delphi developers can utilize code profiling techniques to identify performance bottlenecks within specific code segments or functions. By instrumenting critical sections of code with timing measurements or logging statements, developers can assess the execution time of individual code paths and prioritize optimization efforts accordingly.

delphiCopy code

```
// Example of code profiling in Delphi application var
StartTime, EndTime: TDateTime; begin StartTime :=
Now; // Code segment to profile EndTime := Now;
WriteLn('Execution                    time:                    ',
MilliSecondsBetween(EndTime,        StartTime),        '
milliseconds'); end;
```

By measuring the execution time of specific code segments using timing functions or logging statements, developers can identify performance bottlenecks and focus optimization efforts on areas with the greatest impact on overall application performance.

Furthermore, Delphi applications can benefit from memory profiling techniques to identify memory leaks, excessive memory usage, and inefficient memory management practices. By employing memory profiling tools or libraries, developers can analyze memory allocation patterns, detect memory leaks, and optimize memory usage to improve application stability and performance.

In summary, profiling Delphi applications for performance bottlenecks is a crucial aspect of software development aimed at ensuring optimal application performance and user experience. By leveraging built-in profiling tools, third-party utilities, code profiling techniques, and memory profiling practices, developers can identify performance issues, optimize critical code paths, and deliver high-performance Delphi applications that meet user expectations and performance requirements.

Optimizing code for improved performance is a critical aspect of software development that aims to enhance the efficiency and responsiveness of applications by reducing execution time, minimizing resource consumption, and optimizing critical code paths. In Delphi programming, optimizing code is essential for delivering high-performance applications that meet user expectations and performance requirements. There are various techniques and best practices that Delphi developers can employ to optimize their code and achieve significant performance gains.

One fundamental technique for optimizing code in Delphi is identifying and eliminating performance bottlenecks. Performance bottlenecks are sections of code that significantly impact application performance due to inefficient algorithms, excessive resource usage, or suboptimal coding practices. By utilizing profiling tools and techniques, developers can pinpoint performance bottlenecks and focus optimization efforts on critical code paths that contribute most to overall execution time.

bashCopy code
```
# Example of using a profiler to identify performance
bottlenecks Run the profiler tool on the Delphi
application -> Analyze profiling results to identify
bottlenecks
```

Once performance bottlenecks are identified, developers can employ various optimization techniques to improve code efficiency and execution speed. One such technique is algorithm optimization, which involves replacing inefficient algorithms with more efficient alternatives to reduce computational complexity and improve performance. By selecting the appropriate data structures and algorithms for specific tasks, developers can significantly enhance the performance of their Delphi applications.

delphiCopy code

```
// Example of algorithm optimization in Delphi // Replace bubble sort with quicksort for improved sorting performance procedure QuickSort(var A: array of Integer; Low, High: Integer); begin // Implementation of quicksort algorithm end;
```

In addition to algorithm optimization, Delphi developers can optimize code by minimizing unnecessary resource consumption and reducing memory overhead. Techniques such as object pooling, lazy initialization, and resource caching can help reduce memory usage and improve application performance by minimizing unnecessary object creation and memory allocations.

delphiCopy code

```
// Example of object pooling in Delphi // Reuse objects from a pool instead of creating new ones Object := ObjectPool.AcquireObject; // Use the acquired object ObjectPool.ReleaseObject(Object);
```

Furthermore, optimizing code for improved performance involves leveraging hardware acceleration and parallel processing techniques to maximize the utilization of available system resources. Delphi provides support for multithreading and parallel programming, allowing developers to parallelize computationally intensive tasks and exploit multicore processors for improved performance.

delphiCopy code

```
// Example of parallel processing in Delphi // Parallelize a computationally intensive task using TParallel.For TParallel.For(0, N - 1, procedure(I: Integer) begin // Perform computation for element I end);
```

Another critical aspect of optimizing code in Delphi is reducing function call overhead and minimizing unnecessary code execution. By avoiding unnecessary function calls, reducing function parameter overhead, and optimizing loop structures, developers can achieve significant performance improvements by reducing CPU overhead and minimizing execution time.

delphiCopy code

```
// Example of loop optimization in Delphi // Minimize loop overhead by precalculating loop bounds for I := 0 to High(Array) do begin // Loop body end;
```

Moreover, optimizing code for improved performance involves minimizing disk I/O operations and optimizing database access to reduce latency and improve application responsiveness. Techniques such as batch processing, caching frequently accessed data, and optimizing database queries can help reduce database round trips and improve overall application performance.

```delphi
// Example of optimizing database access in Delphi //
Batch process database queries to minimize round trips
Query := Connection.CreateQuery; Query.SQL.Text :=
'SELECT * FROM Table WHERE Condition'; Query.Open;
while not Query.Eof do begin // Process query results
Query.Next; end;
```

In summary, optimizing code for improved performance is a crucial aspect of Delphi programming aimed at enhancing application efficiency, responsiveness, and scalability. By identifying and eliminating performance bottlenecks, employing algorithm optimization techniques, minimizing resource consumption, leveraging hardware acceleration, and optimizing disk I/O and database access, developers can significantly improve the performance of their Delphi applications and deliver a superior user experience.

Chapter 10: Strategies for Debugging Complex Applications

Debugging large-scale projects presents unique challenges due to the complexity of the codebase, the multitude of interacting components, and the extensive execution paths involved. To effectively debug large-scale projects, developers must employ a combination of techniques and tools tailored to address the specific challenges inherent in such projects.

One essential technique for debugging large-scale projects is using logging and tracing mechanisms to track the flow of execution and capture relevant runtime information. By strategically placing logging statements throughout the codebase and utilizing logging frameworks such as log4delphi or custom logging solutions, developers can gain insights into the internal state of the application and diagnose issues more effectively.

bashCopy code

Example of enabling logging in a large-scale Delphi project Enable logging statements in critical sections of the codebase -> Configure logging framework settings -> Deploy the updated application

Additionally, leveraging version control systems such as Git or SVN can facilitate the debugging process by providing a history of code changes and enabling developers to revert to previous versions for comparison or isolation of issues. By using version control effectively, developers can track down the introduction of bugs, identify changes that may have caused issues, and collaborate with team members to resolve them.

bashCopy code

```
# Example of using Git for debugging in a large-scale
project Checkout previous commits to isolate issues ->
Use git bisect to identify the commit introducing a bug ->
Analyze changes in the problematic commit
```

Furthermore, employing unit testing and integration testing practices can help identify and isolate defects early in the development process, reducing the complexity of debugging in large-scale projects. By writing comprehensive test suites and automating the testing process, developers can validate individual components and ensure their correct behavior within the larger system, thus minimizing the occurrence of bugs in production.

bashCopy code

```
# Example of running unit tests in a large-scale Delphi
project Run unit test suite using a testing framework
such as DUnit -> Analyze test results for failures or errors
-> Debug failing tests to identify underlying issues
```

Moreover, utilizing code analysis tools and static code analysis techniques can assist in identifying potential issues, such as code smells, performance bottlenecks, or violations of coding standards, in large-scale projects. By analyzing the codebase statically, developers can identify areas that require attention and apply refactoring or optimization techniques to improve code quality and maintainability.

bashCopy code

Example of running static code analysis in a large-scale Delphi project Use code analysis tools such as Pascal Analyzer or SonarQube -> Review analysis results for code quality issues -> Address identified issues through refactoring or code changes

In addition to these techniques, employing debugging features provided by integrated development environments (IDEs) such as Delphi can greatly aid in diagnosing issues in large-scale projects. Features such as breakpoints, watchlists, call stacks, and variable inspection tools enable developers to pause execution at specific points, inspect the state of the application, and trace the flow of execution to identify the root cause of issues.

delphiCopy code

// Example of using breakpoints in Delphi IDE for debugging Set breakpoints at critical points in the codebase -> Run the application in debug mode -> Pause execution at breakpoints to inspect variables and trace execution flow

Furthermore, leveraging remote debugging capabilities can be invaluable when debugging large-scale projects deployed on remote servers or devices. By remotely connecting to the target environment and debugging the application in situ, developers can diagnose issues that may only manifest in specific deployment scenarios, thus streamlining the debugging process and accelerating issue resolution.

bashCopy code

Example of remote debugging in a large-scale Delphi project Enable remote debugging support in the Delphi IDE -> Connect to the remote server or device running the

application -> Debug the application remotely using IDE tools

In summary, debugging large-scale projects requires a systematic approach and a combination of techniques tailored to the unique challenges posed by such projects. By leveraging logging and tracing mechanisms, version control systems, testing practices, code analysis tools, IDE features, and remote debugging capabilities, developers can effectively diagnose and resolve issues in large-scale Delphi projects, ensuring the reliability and stability of the final product.

Debugging complex software architectures requires a comprehensive approach that encompasses various strategies and best practices to effectively identify and resolve issues within intricate systems. Complex software architectures often involve multiple layers of abstraction, extensive interactions between components, and dependencies on external systems, making debugging a challenging task. To navigate this complexity successfully, developers must employ a combination of techniques tailored to the specific characteristics of the architecture.

One fundamental best practice for debugging complex software architectures is to establish robust logging and monitoring mechanisms throughout the system. By instrumenting the codebase with logging statements and integrating monitoring tools, developers can gain visibility into the system's behavior, track the flow of data and control, and capture relevant runtime information. This proactive approach allows for the early detection of anomalies, facilitates root cause analysis, and provides valuable insights into system performance and behavior.

```bash
bashCopy code
# Example of enabling logging and monitoring in a
complex software architecture Configure logging
frameworks such as Log4j or ELK stack -> Instrument
codebase with logging statements -> Deploy monitoring
tools for real-time insights
```

Moreover, leveraging debugging tools provided by integrated development environments (IDEs) or specialized debugging platforms is essential for effectively debugging complex software architectures. Features such as breakpoints, watchlists, call stack inspection, and variable inspection tools enable developers to pause execution at critical points, analyze the state of the system, and trace the flow of execution through multiple layers of abstraction. Additionally, advanced debugging features such as conditional breakpoints and remote debugging capabilities can further enhance the debugging process in complex architectures.

```bash
bashCopy code
# Example of using debugging tools in an IDE for complex
software architectures Set breakpoints at critical points in
the codebase -> Utilize watchlists to monitor variable
values -> Analyze call stack to trace execution flow ->
Employ remote debugging for distributed systems
```

Furthermore, employing unit testing and integration testing practices is crucial for validating individual components and verifying their interactions within the broader architecture. By writing comprehensive test suites, developers can verify the correctness of individual modules, detect regressions, and ensure the compatibility and interoperability of components across the system.

Automated testing frameworks and continuous integration pipelines can streamline the testing process, enabling developers to detect and address issues early in the development lifecycle.

bashCopy code

```
# Example of running unit and integration tests in a complex software architecture Execute unit test suite using testing frameworks such as JUnit or NUnit -> Run integration tests to validate component interactions -> Integrate testing into CI/CD pipelines for automated validation
```

Moreover, practicing defensive programming techniques, such as input validation, error handling, and defensive coding practices, is essential for mitigating the impact of potential failures and minimizing the propagation of errors within complex architectures. By anticipating and handling edge cases gracefully, developers can enhance the robustness and resilience of the system, reducing the likelihood of critical failures and improving overall reliability.

bashCopy code

```
# Example of implementing defensive programming in a complex software architecture Validate input data to prevent unexpected behavior -> Implement error handling mechanisms to gracefully handle failures -> Apply defensive coding practices to anticipate potential issues
```

Additionally, adopting a systematic approach to troubleshooting and root cause analysis is crucial for effectively debugging complex software architectures. By following structured methodologies such as the scientific method or root cause analysis frameworks like the 5 Whys, developers can systematically identify, isolate, and resolve issues within the architecture. This approach involves gathering evidence, formulating hypotheses, conducting experiments, and iteratively refining the understanding of the problem until a solution is found.

bashCopy code

Example of applying root cause analysis in debugging complex software architectures Gather evidence and data related to the issue -> Formulate hypotheses about the potential causes -> Conduct experiments to validate hypotheses -> Iterate on the investigation process until the root cause is identified

In summary, debugging complex software architectures requires a multifaceted approach that encompasses logging and monitoring, debugging tools, testing practices, defensive programming, and systematic troubleshooting methodologies. By adopting these best practices and techniques, developers can effectively navigate the intricacies of complex architectures, identify and resolve issues efficiently, and ensure the reliability and stability of the software system.

BOOK 4
DELPHI PASCAL PROGRAMMING PRO
FINE-TUNING CODE EDITING AND VISUAL DESIGNING
FOR EXPERTS

ROB BOTWRIGHT

Chapter 1: Mastering Delphi Pascal's Advanced Editing Features

Exploring advanced text editing tools opens up a world of possibilities for developers, enabling them to streamline their coding workflow, increase productivity, and enhance code quality. These tools go beyond basic text manipulation and provide advanced features tailored to the needs of professional software developers. One such tool is Visual Studio Code (VS Code), a popular integrated development environment (IDE) known for its extensive set of text editing capabilities and rich ecosystem of extensions.

At the core of advanced text editing in VS Code is its powerful editing engine, which supports a wide range of features designed to facilitate code writing, editing, and navigation. One notable feature is IntelliSense, a code completion mechanism that provides context-aware suggestions as developers type, helping them write code faster and with fewer errors. Additionally, VS Code offers sophisticated navigation tools such as Go to Definition and Find All References, allowing developers to quickly navigate to declarations and references within their codebase.

bashCopy code

Example of using IntelliSense in VS Code Ctrl + Space: Trigger IntelliSense suggestions

Another essential aspect of advanced text editing is code refactoring, a process that involves restructuring existing code to improve its readability, maintainability, or performance. VS Code provides built-in support for common refactoring operations such as renaming symbols, extracting code into functions or methods, and reordering function parameters. These refactorings can help developers maintain clean and consistent codebases, reducing the likelihood of bugs and making code easier to understand and maintain.

```bash
bashCopy code
# Example of renaming a symbol in VS Code F2:
Rename symbol under cursor
```

In addition to built-in features, VS Code offers a vast selection of extensions that further enhance its text editing capabilities. These extensions cover a wide range of functionalities, including language support, code linting, formatting, and debugging. For example, extensions like ESLint and Prettier provide automated code formatting and style enforcement, helping developers adhere to coding standards and best practices.

```bash
bashCopy code
# Example of installing an extension in VS Code Ctrl + Shift + X: Open Extensions view
```

Moreover, advanced text editing tools often include support for version control systems, enabling developers to manage changes to their codebase effectively. VS Code integrates seamlessly with popular version control systems such as Git, providing features like inline git blame annotations, commit history exploration, and conflict resolution tools. These features empower developers to collaborate more efficiently and maintain a clear history of changes to their codebase.

bashCopy code

Example of using Git commands in VS Code Ctrl + Shift + G: Open Source Control view

Furthermore, advanced text editing tools often offer extensive customization options, allowing developers to tailor the IDE to their specific preferences and workflows. In VS Code, users can customize keybindings, themes, and editor settings through a user-friendly interface or by editing configuration files directly. This flexibility enables developers to create a personalized coding environment that maximizes their productivity and comfort.

bashCopy code

Example of customizing keybindings in VS Code Ctrl + K, Ctrl + S: Open Keyboard Shortcuts settings

Additionally, modern text editing tools leverage the power of artificial intelligence and machine learning to provide intelligent code suggestions and automated code generation. VS Code's AI-powered IntelliCode feature analyzes patterns in a developer's codebase and provides context-aware recommendations to improve productivity and code quality. These AI-driven capabilities help developers write code faster and with greater confidence, reducing the cognitive load associated with manual code writing.

bashCopy code

```
# Example of using IntelliCode suggestions in VS Code
Ctrl + Space: Trigger IntelliSense suggestions enhanced
with AI
```

In summary, exploring advanced text editing tools like Visual Studio Code empowers developers to take their coding skills to the next level. By leveraging powerful editing features, code refactoring capabilities, extensions, version control integration, customization options, and AI-driven assistance, developers can streamline their workflow, write cleaner and more maintainable code, and ultimately deliver higher-quality software products.

Utilizing advanced search and navigation features within integrated development environments (IDEs) like Visual Studio Code (VS Code) significantly enhances developers' efficiency and productivity. These features allow developers to navigate through codebases swiftly, locate specific pieces of code, and understand code structures more comprehensively. VS Code, with its robust set of search and navigation capabilities, provides developers with powerful tools to streamline their workflow and improve code exploration.

One fundamental feature of advanced search and navigation in VS Code is the ability to search for symbols within a project or workspace. This feature enables developers to quickly locate classes, functions, variables, and other symbols across multiple files. By utilizing the "Go to Symbol" command, developers can access a list of symbols within the current file or navigate directly to a specific symbol by typing its name.

bashCopy code

Ctrl + Shift + O: Open symbol list for the current file Ctrl + Shift + P, then type "Go to Symbol": Navigate to a symbol by name

Furthermore, VS Code offers powerful search capabilities through its integrated search functionality. The "Find" feature allows developers to search for text within the current file or across the entire workspace, supporting both simple text searches and regular expressions. Additionally, the "Find in Files" feature extends the search scope to include all files within the workspace, enabling developers to perform comprehensive searches for specific patterns or expressions.

bashCopy code

Ctrl + F: Open the Find widget for searching within the current file Ctrl + Shift + F: Open the Find in Files view for searching across the entire workspace

Another essential aspect of advanced navigation in VS Code is the ability to navigate through code structures effectively. The "Go to Definition" command allows developers to navigate to the definition of a symbol, such as a function or class, within the current file or across the entire project. This feature provides valuable insights into how different components of the codebase are implemented and interconnected.

bashCopy code

F12: Go to the definition of the symbol under the cursor Ctrl + Click: Navigate to the definition of the symbol under the cursor

Moreover, VS Code supports advanced navigation through references, enabling developers to find all references to a particular symbol within the codebase. By using the "Find All References" command, developers can view a list of all locations where a symbol is referenced, allowing them to understand its usage and context more thoroughly.

bashCopy code

Shift + F12: Find all references to the symbol under the cursor

Additionally, VS Code provides valuable insights into code structure and dependencies through its integrated "Peek Definition" and "Peek References" features. These features allow developers to view the definition or references of a symbol directly within the current file, without navigating away from the original context. This inline preview capability streamlines the code exploration process and helps developers maintain focus on their current tasks.

bashCopy code

Alt + F12: Peek definition of the symbol under the cursor Shift + F12 (with the cursor on a symbol): Peek references to the symbol

Furthermore, VS Code offers seamless integration with version control systems like Git, enhancing code navigation capabilities within the context of code changes and history. Developers can use commands such as "Git: Open Changes" and "Git: Open File" to navigate through the changes made to a file or explore its history, facilitating code review and collaboration workflows.

bashCopy code

Ctrl + Shift + G: Open the Source Control view for Git commands

In summary, utilizing advanced search and navigation features in Visual Studio Code empowers developers to navigate through codebases efficiently, locate specific pieces of code, and understand code structures more comprehensively. By leveraging commands such as "Go to Symbol," "Find in Files," "Go to Definition," and "Find All References," developers can streamline their workflow, increase productivity, and gain valuable insights into code dependencies and usage patterns.

Chapter 2: Leveraging Code Templates and Snippets for Efficiency

Creating and managing code templates is an essential aspect of modern software development workflows, enabling developers to streamline their coding process, maintain consistency, and improve productivity. In integrated development environments (IDEs) like Visual Studio Code (VS Code), the ability to create and manage code templates provides developers with a powerful toolset to automate repetitive tasks, standardize coding practices, and accelerate development cycles.

The process of creating code templates typically involves defining reusable snippets of code that can be easily inserted into new or existing files. These templates often include common code structures, such as function definitions, class declarations, method signatures, or code comments, tailored to specific programming languages or frameworks. By defining these templates, developers can eliminate the need to manually type boilerplate code, reducing the likelihood of errors and enhancing code consistency across projects.

In VS Code, creating and managing code templates can be accomplished using the built-in "User Snippets" feature, which allows developers to define custom snippets for various programming languages. To create a new code template, developers can navigate to the "User Snippets" section within the IDE settings and select the desired language for which they want to define a snippet. For example, to define a new snippet for JavaScript, developers can open the JavaScript language settings and create a new snippet file.

bashCopy code

Ctrl + Shift + P, then type "Preferences: Configure User Snippets" : Open the User Snippets settings

Once in the snippet file, developers can define their custom code templates using a simple JSON-based syntax. Each snippet consists of a unique identifier, a prefix (the text that triggers the snippet), and a body (the code content of the snippet). Additionally, developers can include placeholders within the snippet body to dynamically insert variable content, such as variable names or function parameters, at the time of insertion.

jsonCopy code

{ "My Custom Snippet": { "prefix": "mySnippet", "body": ["console.log('This is my custom snippet');"], "description": "A custom snippet example" } }

Once defined, these code templates are readily accessible within the IDE, allowing developers to insert them into their code with a simple keystroke or command. By typing the snippet prefix and pressing the associated key binding or selecting the snippet from the IntelliSense suggestions, developers can quickly insert the predefined code template into their files, saving time and effort.

In addition to creating custom code templates, developers can also leverage existing snippet libraries and extensions provided by the VS Code community.

These libraries often include a wide range of pre-defined snippets for popular programming languages, frameworks, and libraries, covering common use cases and coding patterns. By installing these extensions, developers can expand their snippet repertoire and take advantage of ready-to-use templates for various scenarios.

Moreover, VS Code offers advanced features for managing and organizing code snippets, allowing developers to categorize snippets into different groups or folders for better organization and accessibility. By grouping related snippets together, developers can easily navigate and discover relevant templates based on their specific use cases or project requirements, further enhancing productivity and workflow efficiency.

Furthermore, VS Code supports the sharing and syncing of code snippets across multiple development environments through various mechanisms such as version control systems, cloud storage services, or built-in synchronization features. By storing snippet files in a shared repository or syncing them using cloud storage providers like GitHub or Dropbox, developers can ensure consistent access to their custom templates across different machines and development environments.

In summary, creating and managing code templates in Visual Studio Code is a valuable practice for improving developer productivity, maintaining code consistency, and streamlining the coding process. By defining custom snippets, leveraging existing snippet libraries, organizing snippets into groups, and sharing snippets across environments, developers can optimize their workflow, reduce repetitive tasks, and focus on writing high-quality code.

Increasing productivity with code snippets is a fundamental aspect of modern software development, providing developers with a powerful mechanism to automate repetitive tasks, accelerate coding workflows, and maintain consistency across projects. Code snippets, short and reusable pieces of code, offer a convenient way to insert commonly used code patterns, templates, or structures into source files with minimal effort, reducing manual typing and saving valuable time during development.

In integrated development environments (IDEs) like Visual Studio Code (VS Code), code snippets are a built-in feature designed to enhance developer productivity. By leveraging code snippets, developers can streamline their coding process and focus on solving complex problems rather than writing boilerplate code. VS Code provides robust support for creating, managing, and using code snippets across various programming languages and frameworks, making it an indispensable tool for developers looking to optimize their workflow.

To create a new code snippet in VS Code, developers can utilize the "User Snippets" feature, which allows them to define custom snippets for specific programming languages or frameworks. By opening the user snippets settings for a particular language, developers can create a new snippet file or modify an existing one to include their custom code templates.

bashCopy code

Ctrl + Shift + P, then type "Preferences: Configure User Snippets": Open the User Snippets settings

Once in the snippet file, developers can define their custom code snippets using a simple JSON-based syntax. Each snippet consists of a unique identifier, a prefix (the text that triggers the snippet), and a body (the code content of the snippet). Additionally, developers can include placeholders within the snippet body to dynamically insert variable content, such as variable names or function parameters, at the time of insertion.

jsonCopy code

```json
{ "My Custom Snippet": { "prefix": "mySnippet", "body": [ "console.log('This is my custom snippet');" ], "description": "A custom snippet example" } }
```

Once defined, these code snippets become readily accessible within the IDE, allowing developers to insert them into their code with a simple keystroke or command. By typing the snippet prefix and pressing the associated key binding or selecting the snippet from the IntelliSense suggestions, developers can quickly insert the predefined code template into their files, saving time and effort.

Moreover, developers can leverage existing snippet libraries and extensions provided by the VS Code community to further enhance their productivity. These libraries often include a wide range of pre-defined snippets for popular programming languages, frameworks, and libraries, covering common use cases and coding patterns. By installing these extensions, developers can expand their snippet repertoire and take advantage of ready-to-use templates for various scenarios.

In addition to creating custom code snippets, developers can also customize and extend existing snippets to better suit their specific needs. VS Code allows developers to modify snippet files directly within the IDE, enabling them to add new snippets, update existing ones, or remove snippets that are no longer needed. By tailoring snippets to match their coding style and preferences, developers can further optimize their workflow and reduce the time spent on repetitive tasks.

Furthermore, VS Code offers advanced features for managing and organizing code snippets, allowing developers to categorize snippets into different groups or folders for better organization and accessibility. By grouping related snippets together, developers can easily navigate and discover relevant templates based on their specific use cases or project requirements, further enhancing productivity and workflow efficiency.

In summary, code snippets are invaluable tools for increasing productivity and efficiency in software development. By creating, managing, and using code snippets effectively, developers can streamline their coding process, reduce manual typing, and focus on writing high-quality code. With the robust support for code snippets provided by VS Code and the extensive ecosystem of snippet libraries and extensions available, developers have everything they need to maximize their productivity and achieve their coding goals.

Chapter 3: Customizing the IDE for Maximum Productivity

Customizing editor settings and preferences is a crucial aspect of modern software development, enabling developers to tailor their coding environment to suit their individual preferences, coding style, and workflow requirements. In integrated development environments (IDEs) like Visual Studio Code (VS Code), customization options abound, allowing developers to adjust various aspects of the editor's behavior, appearance, and functionality to optimize their coding experience.

To begin customizing editor settings and preferences in VS Code, developers can access the settings menu by navigating to the "File" menu and selecting "Preferences," followed by "Settings," or by using the shortcut:

bashCopy code

Ctrl + ,

This command opens the settings view, where developers can configure a wide range of options to personalize their coding environment. The settings view in VS Code is divided into two main sections: user settings and workspace settings. User settings apply globally to all projects, while workspace settings are specific to the current project and override user settings when present.

Within the settings view, developers can modify editor preferences such as indentation settings, tab size, line wrapping behavior, font family, font size, and theme. By adjusting these settings to match their personal preferences and coding style, developers can create a more comfortable and visually appealing coding environment.

For example, to change the default font family and size in VS Code, developers can search for the "Editor: Font Family" and "Editor: Font Size" settings in the settings view and specify their desired font family and size values. Additionally, developers can install custom themes from the VS Code marketplace to further customize the appearance of the editor and make it more visually appealing.

In addition to modifying editor appearance, developers can also customize various behavior settings to enhance their productivity and workflow efficiency. For instance, developers can configure settings related to auto save behavior, file associations, file encoding, and line ending preferences to align with their workflow requirements.

Moreover, VS Code offers extensive support for key bindings customization, allowing developers to define custom key bindings for frequently used commands or actions. By accessing the keyboard shortcuts settings, developers can create, modify, or remove key bindings to streamline their workflow and perform common tasks more efficiently.

Furthermore, VS Code provides powerful extension capabilities that enable developers to extend the editor's functionality and add new features through the installation of extensions from the VS Code marketplace. These extensions can range from language support, code snippets, linters, and debuggers to project management tools, version control integrations, and beyond.

By installing relevant extensions, developers can augment their coding environment with additional capabilities tailored to their specific needs and preferences. For example, developers working with specific programming languages or frameworks can install language-specific extensions to benefit from enhanced syntax highlighting, code completion, and error checking features.

Additionally, developers can leverage productivity-focused extensions such as GitLens for Git version control integration, Prettier for code formatting, ESLint for JavaScript linting, and Bracket Pair Colorizer for improved code readability. These extensions not only enhance the development experience but also promote coding best practices and standards adherence.

Moreover, developers can share their customized editor settings and preferences with team members by saving them as workspace settings or exporting them as a settings file. This ensures consistency across team members' coding environments and facilitates collaboration on shared projects.

In summary, customizing editor settings and preferences in VS Code is essential for creating a personalized and efficient coding environment tailored to individual preferences and workflow requirements. By adjusting editor appearance, behavior, key bindings, and installing relevant extensions, developers can optimize their productivity, enhance their coding experience, and streamline their workflow in VS Code.

Personalizing the layout of an integrated development environment (IDE) and managing tool windows are fundamental aspects of creating a conducive coding environment that aligns with developers' preferences and workflows. In modern IDEs like IntelliJ IDEA, JetBrains' flagship IDE for Java development, customization options abound, empowering developers to tailor their workspace layout and tool window configuration to suit their individual needs and enhance their productivity.

To begin personalizing the IDE layout and managing tool windows in IntelliJ IDEA, developers can utilize various commands accessible from the IDE's menus or by using keyboard shortcuts. For instance, to customize the layout of the IDE's main window, developers can navigate to the "Window" menu and select options such as "Editor Tabs" or "Tool Windows" to toggle the visibility of specific components or rearrange them according to their preferences. Additionally, developers can use the following command to open the "Tool Windows" menu:

bashCopy code

Alt + Shift + F12

This command opens a dropdown menu displaying a list of available tool windows in IntelliJ IDEA, allowing developers to quickly access and manage tool windows such as the Project tool window, Version Control tool window, Run tool window, and many others. By selecting or deselecting specific tool windows from this menu, developers can customize the layout of their workspace to focus on the tools and information relevant to their current task.

Furthermore, IntelliJ IDEA offers a wide range of predefined IDE layouts, or "perspectives," optimized for specific development tasks or programming languages. Developers can switch between different perspectives using the following command:

bashCopy code

Ctrl + F12

This command opens a dropdown menu displaying available perspectives, allowing developers to quickly switch between perspectives tailored to tasks such as coding, debugging, version control, or database development. Each perspective comes with a predefined layout and set of visible tool windows optimized for the selected task, enabling developers to streamline their workflow and maximize productivity.

Moreover, IntelliJ IDEA provides extensive support for customizing the arrangement and appearance of tool windows within the IDE's main window. Developers can drag and drop tool windows to rearrange them, dock tool windows to different edges of the main window, or detach tool windows to float freely as separate windows outside the main IDE frame. Additionally, developers can resize tool windows by dragging their borders or collapse tool windows to conserve screen space when not in use.

In addition to arranging tool windows within the main IDE window, IntelliJ IDEA allows developers to create and manage multiple tool window layouts, known as "layouts," to accommodate different development tasks or project contexts. Developers can save and switch between different layouts using the "Manage IDE Settings" dialog accessible from the "File" menu or by using the following command:

bashCopy code

Ctrl + Alt + S

This command opens the "Settings" dialog, where developers can navigate to the "Appearance & Behavior" section and select "Window Options" to manage tool window layouts. From the "Window Options" menu, developers can save the current layout as a new custom layout, import or export layouts, or switch between saved layouts.

Furthermore, IntelliJ IDEA provides various options for fine-tuning the behavior and appearance of individual tool windows, allowing developers to customize tool window settings according to their preferences. For example, developers can configure auto-hide behavior, adjust tool window width or height, or change the placement of tool window tabs within the main window.

In summary, personalizing the IDE layout and managing tool windows in IntelliJ IDEA is essential for creating a comfortable and efficient coding environment tailored to developers' preferences and workflows. By leveraging commands, menus, and dialogues provided by IntelliJ IDEA, developers can customize the arrangement, appearance, and behavior of tool windows to optimize their productivity and enhance their development experience.

Chapter 4: Harnessing the Power of Refactoring in Delphi Pascal

Understanding refactoring principles is crucial for developers aiming to improve the structure, readability, and maintainability of their codebases over time. Refactoring refers to the process of restructuring existing code without changing its external behavior to make it easier to understand, modify, and maintain. By adhering to refactoring principles, developers can effectively manage technical debt, reduce code complexity, and enhance the overall quality of their software projects.

One of the fundamental principles of refactoring is the idea of incremental changes. Rather than attempting to refactor large portions of code in a single step, developers should break down refactoring tasks into smaller, manageable steps and apply changes gradually. This approach minimizes the risk of introducing bugs or regressions while making it easier to verify that each refactoring step preserves the correct behavior of the code.

To apply the principle of incremental changes effectively, developers can utilize various refactoring techniques provided by modern integrated development environments (IDEs) or code editors. For example, popular IDEs such as JetBrains IntelliJ IDEA or Microsoft Visual Studio offer built-in support for a wide range of refactoring operations, including extracting methods, renaming variables, and introducing new abstractions. By using these tools, developers can refactor code more efficiently and with greater confidence, knowing that the IDE will help them maintain code consistency and correctness throughout the process.

Another essential principle of refactoring is the concept of preserving code semantics. When refactoring code, developers must ensure that the behavior of the code remains unchanged after applying refactoring transformations. This principle emphasizes the importance of thorough testing and validation to verify that refactored code behaves as expected under various scenarios and edge cases. By writing automated tests and performing manual inspections, developers can detect and address any unintended side effects introduced by refactoring changes, thus maintaining the reliability and correctness of the codebase.

In addition to preserving code semantics, refactoring should also aim to improve code readability and maintainability. This involves eliminating code smells, such as duplicated code, long methods, or excessive complexity, that can hinder understanding and modification of the codebase. By applying refactoring techniques such as extracting methods, splitting classes, or introducing design patterns, developers can make code easier to comprehend, navigate, and extend, leading to improved developer productivity and reduced likelihood of introducing bugs during future development efforts.

Furthermore, refactoring principles emphasize the importance of continuous improvement and evolution of the codebase. Software projects are dynamic entities that evolve over time in response to changing requirements, technologies, and business needs. As such, refactoring should be viewed as an ongoing process rather than a one-time activity. By regularly reviewing and refactoring code as part of the development workflow, developers can ensure that the codebase remains clean, maintainable, and adaptable to future changes, thus mitigating the accumulation of technical debt and minimizing the risk of software stagnation or obsolescence.

Moreover, refactoring principles encourage collaboration and knowledge sharing among team members. Refactoring should not be seen as the sole responsibility of individual developers but rather as a collective effort aimed at improving the overall quality and sustainability of the codebase. By fostering a culture of code reviews, pair programming, and continuous feedback, teams can leverage the diverse expertise and perspectives of team members to identify refactoring opportunities, prioritize refactoring tasks, and ensure that refactoring efforts align with the project's goals and objectives.

Additionally, refactoring principles emphasize the importance of documentation and communication when making changes to the codebase. Developers should document the rationale behind refactoring decisions, as well as any potential trade-offs or considerations that may impact the codebase's behavior or performance. By maintaining clear and up-to-date documentation, developers can facilitate knowledge transfer, reduce the learning curve for new team members, and ensure that refactoring efforts are well-informed and aligned with the project's long-term vision and roadmap.

Furthermore, refactoring principles advocate for the use of code metrics and static analysis tools to identify areas of the codebase that would benefit most from refactoring. By analyzing code complexity, coupling, and cohesion metrics, developers can pinpoint potential code smells and hotspots that require attention and prioritize refactoring efforts accordingly. Additionally, static analysis tools can automatically detect common code issues and suggest refactoring opportunities, thereby augmenting developers' ability to maintain code quality and consistency across the codebase.

In summary, understanding refactoring principles is essential for developers seeking to improve the quality, maintainability, and longevity of their software projects. By adhering to principles such as incremental changes, preserving code semantics, improving readability and maintainability, fostering collaboration and communication, and leveraging code metrics and static analysis tools, developers can effectively refactor codebases to keep them clean, efficient, and adaptable to changing requirements and environments. By making refactoring an integral part of the development process, teams can cultivate a culture of continuous improvement and deliver high-quality software that meets the needs of stakeholders and users alike.

Applying refactoring techniques in Delphi projects is essential for maintaining code quality, improving readability, and ensuring the long-term maintainability of software applications. Refactoring involves making systematic changes to the structure of code without altering its external behavior, with the goal of simplifying complexity, reducing duplication, and enhancing overall code maintainability.

One of the most commonly used refactoring techniques in Delphi projects is method extraction, which involves identifying and isolating a segment of code within a method and extracting it into a separate method. This helps improve code readability, promotes code reuse, and makes methods more focused and easier to understand. In Delphi, the Extract Method refactoring can be applied using the built-in refactoring tools available in the IDE. For example, to extract a method in Delphi, developers can select the code block they want to extract, right-click, and choose the "Refactor" option from the context menu, followed by "Extract Method."

Another useful refactoring technique in Delphi projects is method parameterization, which involves replacing hardcoded values or constants within a method with parameters, making the method more flexible and reusable. Parameterization allows developers to customize the behavior of a method without modifying its implementation, enhancing code flexibility and extensibility. To apply method parameterization in Delphi, developers can use the "Extract Parameter" refactoring provided by the IDE, which allows them to select a constant or value within a method, right-click, and choose the "Refactor" option followed by "Extract Parameter."

In addition to method extraction and parameterization, Delphi developers can also benefit from refactoring techniques such as method renaming, which involves renaming methods to better reflect their purpose or functionality. Renaming methods using descriptive and meaningful names can improve code readability and comprehension, making it easier for developers to understand the intent of each method. In Delphi, developers can rename methods using the "Rename" refactoring provided by the IDE, which automatically updates all references to the method throughout the codebase.

Furthermore, Delphi projects can benefit from refactoring techniques aimed at improving code structure and organization, such as class extraction and decomposition. Class extraction involves identifying cohesive sets of functionality within existing classes and extracting them into separate classes, promoting code modularity and separation of concerns. Decomposition involves breaking down large and complex classes into smaller, more manageable components, reducing code complexity and improving maintainability. To perform class extraction or decomposition in Delphi, developers can use the "Extract Class" or "Extract Interface" refactoring options provided by the IDE, respectively.

Moreover, Delphi developers can leverage refactoring techniques to address code smells and improve code quality. Code smells are indicators of potential design or implementation issues in code, such as duplication, excessive complexity, or tight coupling. By applying refactoring techniques such as code deduplication, method consolidation, or class restructuring, developers can eliminate code smells and improve overall code quality and maintainability. Delphi provides a range of built-in refactoring tools and IDE features that support these refactoring operations, allowing developers to refactor code efficiently and effectively.

Additionally, Delphi projects can benefit from refactoring techniques aimed at improving code performance and efficiency. Performance-related refactorings involve optimizing code to reduce execution time, memory usage, or resource consumption, improving overall application performance. Techniques such as loop unrolling, algorithm optimization, or data structure redesign can help optimize critical sections of code and enhance application performance. Delphi developers can use profiling tools and performance analysis features provided by the IDE to identify performance bottlenecks and apply appropriate refactoring techniques to address them.

Furthermore, Delphi projects can benefit from refactoring techniques aimed at enhancing code maintainability and scalability. Scalability-related refactorings involve designing code in a way that allows it to accommodate future changes, additions, or enhancements without requiring extensive rework. Techniques such as modularization, abstraction, or encapsulation can help improve code maintainability and scalability by isolating dependencies, promoting code reuse, and minimizing the impact of changes. Delphi developers can use refactoring tools and design patterns to refactor code in a way that makes it more adaptable and extensible, ensuring its long-term viability and sustainability.

In summary, applying refactoring techniques in Delphi projects is essential for maintaining code quality, improving readability, and ensuring the long-term maintainability and scalability of software applications. By leveraging built-in refactoring tools and IDE features, Delphi developers can refactor code efficiently and effectively, addressing code smells, optimizing performance, and promoting code modularity and reusability. By making refactoring an integral part of the development process, Delphi projects can deliver high-quality, reliable, and maintainable software that meets the needs of stakeholders and users alike.

Chapter 5: Advanced Techniques in Visual Designing with Delphi Forms

Advanced layout and alignment strategies play a pivotal role in designing user interfaces that are not only visually appealing but also intuitive and user-friendly. As software applications become more complex and diverse in functionality, employing advanced techniques for layout and alignment becomes increasingly important to ensure that the user experience remains consistent and cohesive across different devices and screen sizes.

One of the fundamental aspects of advanced layout and alignment strategies is understanding the principles of responsive design. Responsive design aims to create interfaces that adapt fluidly to various screen sizes and orientations, providing users with an optimal viewing experience on any device, whether it's a desktop computer, tablet, or smartphone. To achieve responsive layouts in web development, developers often utilize CSS media queries to adjust the styling and layout of elements based on factors such as screen width, height, and aspect ratio. For example, a media query command in CSS can be used to set different styles for elements when the screen width is below a certain threshold, allowing for the creation of mobile-friendly layouts.

In addition to responsive design principles, advanced layout and alignment strategies also involve mastering advanced CSS techniques such as flexbox and grid layout. Flexbox, short for flexible box layout, is a CSS layout model that allows developers to design complex layouts with ease by providing a more efficient way to align and distribute space among items within a container. With flexbox, developers can specify how items should behave in terms of size, alignment, and order, making it ideal for creating responsive and dynamic layouts. For instance, the display: flex command in CSS can be used to enable flexbox layout for a container element, allowing its child elements to be arranged horizontally or vertically based on the specified flex direction.

Similarly, CSS grid layout is another powerful tool for creating complex and grid-based layouts in web development. Unlike flexbox, which focuses on arranging items along a single axis (either horizontally or vertically), CSS grid layout allows developers to create two-dimensional grid layouts with rows and columns, providing more control over the placement and alignment of elements within the grid. By defining grid tracks, grid lines, and grid areas, developers can create highly customizable layouts that adapt to different screen sizes and content requirements. For example, the display: grid command in CSS can be used to enable grid layout for a container element, allowing developers to define the structure of the grid and the placement of its child elements using grid-specific properties such as grid-template-rows, grid-template-columns, and grid-gap.

Moreover, advanced layout and alignment strategies often involve the use of CSS frameworks and libraries that provide pre-designed components and utilities for building responsive and visually appealing interfaces. Popular CSS frameworks such as Bootstrap, Foundation, and Materialize offer a wide range of components, grid systems, and responsive utilities that simplify the process of designing and styling layouts, allowing developers to focus more on functionality and less on repetitive styling tasks. By leveraging these frameworks, developers can expedite the development process and ensure consistency and compatibility across different browsers and devices.

Furthermore, advanced layout and alignment strategies extend beyond CSS and encompass other design principles and techniques such as typography, color theory, and visual hierarchy. Typography, for example, plays a crucial role in enhancing readability and accessibility in user interfaces by carefully selecting fonts, font sizes, and line heights that complement the overall design aesthetic. Similarly, color theory principles can be applied to create visually harmonious color palettes that convey the desired mood or tone and improve the overall user experience. Additionally, understanding visual hierarchy and the principles of information architecture can help developers organize and prioritize content effectively, guiding users' attention and facilitating navigation within the interface.

In summary, advanced layout and alignment strategies are essential for creating modern, responsive, and visually compelling user interfaces that meet the needs and expectations of users in today's digital landscape.

By mastering responsive design principles, leveraging advanced CSS techniques such as flexbox and grid layout, and incorporating design principles such as typography and color theory, developers can design interfaces that are not only aesthetically pleasing but also intuitive, accessible, and user-friendly. Moreover, by utilizing CSS frameworks and libraries, developers can streamline the development process and ensure consistency and compatibility across different devices and platforms, ultimately delivering a superior user experience.

Creating customized user interface (UI) elements is a crucial aspect of modern software development, allowing developers to tailor the look and feel of their applications to meet specific design requirements and enhance the overall user experience. Whether it's designing unique buttons, customizing form controls, or creating interactive elements, the ability to craft customized UI components is essential for creating visually appealing and highly functional applications.

One of the primary techniques for creating customized UI elements is leveraging HTML and CSS to style standard HTML elements or create entirely custom components from scratch. CSS, or Cascading Style Sheets, provides developers with a wide range of styling options to modify the appearance of HTML elements, including fonts, colors, sizes, borders, and backgrounds. By applying CSS rules and properties selectively, developers can achieve a wide variety of visual effects and design styles, ranging from minimalist and flat designs to more elaborate and intricate layouts.

For example, to create a customized button with a unique color scheme and hover effect, developers can use CSS to define the button's background color, text color, padding, border radius, and transition properties. By specifying different styles for the button's default, hover, active, and focus states, developers can create a visually appealing and interactive button that enhances the overall user experience. Additionally, CSS preprocessors such as Sass and Less can further streamline the process of creating and managing complex CSS stylesheets by introducing features such as variables, mixins, and nested rules.

In addition to CSS, JavaScript plays a crucial role in creating dynamic and interactive UI elements that respond to user input and interaction. With JavaScript, developers can add behavior and functionality to HTML elements, such as handling click events, animating transitions, and updating content dynamically. By combining JavaScript with CSS, developers can create sophisticated UI components, such as sliders, tabs, accordions, and modal dialogs, that enhance the usability and interactivity of their applications.

For example, to create a custom dropdown menu that displays additional options when clicked, developers can use JavaScript to toggle the visibility of the menu's dropdown content based on the user's interaction with the menu button. By adding event listeners to the menu button and dropdown content, developers can define the behavior of the dropdown menu, such as opening and closing animations, keyboard accessibility, and focus management. Additionally, JavaScript frameworks and libraries such as jQuery, React, Vue.js, and Angular provide developers with pre-built components and utilities for creating interactive UI elements more efficiently.

Furthermore, the advent of modern web technologies such as CSS3 and HTML5 has enabled developers to create even more advanced and visually stunning UI elements using techniques such as animations, transitions, and transformations. CSS3 introduces powerful features such as keyframe animations, transitions, and transforms, which allow developers to create fluid and expressive animations that enhance the user experience. By defining custom animation sequences, easing functions, and timing parameters, developers can create engaging and interactive UI elements that capture users' attention and provide feedback in real-time.

For instance, to create a custom loading spinner that animates while content is being fetched from a server, developers can use CSS keyframe animations to define the spinner's rotation and scale transformations over time. By applying these animations to a circular element using CSS classes and selectors, developers can create a visually appealing loading indicator that communicates to users that the application is in progress. Additionally, CSS transitions can be used to add smooth and gradual changes to CSS properties, such as opacity, width, height, and color, in response to user interactions or state changes.

Moreover, the rise of front-end development frameworks such as Bootstrap, Materialize, and Foundation has democratized the process of creating customized UI elements by providing developers with a wide range of pre-designed components, templates, and stylesheets that can be easily customized and extended to suit specific design requirements. These frameworks offer a comprehensive set of UI components, including buttons, forms, navigation bars, cards, and modals, that adhere to best practices in usability, accessibility, and responsive design. By leveraging these frameworks, developers can accelerate the development process and ensure consistency and compatibility across different devices and browsers.

In summary, creating customized UI elements is an essential skill for modern software developers seeking to create visually appealing and highly functional applications. By combining HTML, CSS, and JavaScript, developers can design and implement a wide variety of UI components that enhance the overall user experience and differentiate their applications from the competition. Whether it's leveraging CSS for styling and layout, JavaScript for interactivity and behavior, or modern web technologies for animations and transitions, the ability to create customized UI elements is crucial for delivering compelling and engaging user interfaces in today's digital landscape.

Chapter 6: Creating Custom Components and Controls

Developing custom components in Delphi is a fundamental aspect of creating robust and feature-rich applications tailored to specific requirements. Delphi, known for its powerful integrated development environment (IDE) and component-based architecture, provides developers with the tools and framework necessary to design, build, and deploy custom components efficiently.

The process of developing custom components in Delphi typically begins with identifying the need for a specialized functionality or user interface element that is not readily available in the standard component palette. This could range from complex data visualization controls to simple utility components designed to streamline common tasks. Once the requirements for the custom component are defined, developers can leverage Delphi's component framework to create the desired functionality.

One of the primary tools for developing custom components in Delphi is the Component Designer, which is integrated into the Delphi IDE. The Component Designer allows developers to visually design and configure components using a drag-and-drop interface, making it easy to arrange and customize the appearance and behavior of the component. Developers can add properties, events, and methods to the component, define default values, and set design-time properties to customize the component's appearance and behavior in the IDE.

To create a custom component in Delphi, developers typically start by creating a new unit in the Delphi project and defining a new class that inherits from an existing component class or one of the built-in Delphi component classes, such as TComponent or TControl. The new class serves as the blueprint for the custom component and determines its properties, methods, and events. Developers can then override and extend the default behavior of the base class to implement the desired functionality.

For example, to create a custom button component with additional features such as custom captions, colors, and mouse hover effects, developers can define a new class that inherits from the TButton class and override the Paint method to customize the button's appearance. By adding new properties such as CaptionColor and HoverColor, developers can expose these customization options to users of the custom component, allowing them to tailor the button's appearance to their preferences.

In addition to the Component Designer, Delphi provides developers with a powerful set of tools and libraries for building custom components, including the Visual Component Library (VCL) and the FireMonkey framework. The VCL is a comprehensive set of visual and non-visual components designed for building Windows-based applications, while FireMonkey is a cross-platform UI framework that supports building applications for Windows, macOS, iOS, and Android.

Developers can leverage the VCL or FireMonkey framework to create custom components that are compatible with their target platform and provide a consistent user experience across different devices and operating systems. By utilizing the rich set of components and controls provided by Delphi, developers can focus on implementing the core functionality of the custom component without having to worry about low-level details such as platform-specific APIs and libraries.

To deploy custom components in Delphi, developers typically package them into runtime packages (.bpl files) that can be dynamically linked to Delphi projects at design time or runtime. This allows developers to reuse and share custom components across multiple projects without having to recompile or redistribute the entire application. Additionally, developers can distribute custom components as standalone units (.pas files) or install them into the Delphi IDE using the Component Palette, making them readily available for use in new projects.

Overall, developing custom components in Delphi is a versatile and powerful approach to extending the functionality of Delphi applications and creating unique user experiences. By leveraging the Component Designer, the VCL or FireMonkey framework, and Delphi's component-based architecture, developers can design, build, and deploy custom components with ease, enhancing the productivity and efficiency of their development workflow. Whether it's creating custom user interface controls, data visualization components, or utility classes, Delphi provides developers with the tools and flexibility to bring their ideas to life and deliver high-quality software solutions. Extending built-in controls for specialized functionality is a crucial aspect of software development, particularly in environments like Delphi where customization is key to creating tailored user experiences. Delphi provides developers with a rich set of built-in controls that cover a wide range of functionalities, from simple buttons and text boxes to more complex data grids and charts. However, there are often scenarios where the standard controls do not fully meet the requirements of an application, necessitating the need for customizations and extensions.

In Delphi, extending built-in controls for specialized functionality involves leveraging the object-oriented nature of the language to subclass existing controls and add new features or behavior. This approach allows developers to build upon the foundation provided by the standard controls while retaining their familiar properties, methods, and events. By extending built-in controls, developers can create custom components that seamlessly integrate with existing codebases and provide the specific functionality required for their applications.

One common scenario where extending built-in controls is necessary is when developers need to enhance the visual appearance or behavior of standard controls to better suit the requirements of their application. For example, developers may need to create a custom button control that displays an animated icon or tooltip when hovered over, or a custom text box control that supports advanced formatting options such as syntax highlighting or auto-completion.

To extend built-in controls in Delphi, developers typically start by creating a new class that inherits from the base class of the control they want to extend. For example, to create a custom button control, developers would create a new class that inherits from the TButton class. They can then override and extend the default behavior of the base class by adding new properties, methods, and events to implement the specialized functionality.

Once the custom control class is defined, developers can use it in their Delphi projects just like any other built-in control. They can place instances of the custom control on forms or data modules using the Delphi IDE's design-time editor, and they can interact with the control programmatically by accessing its properties and methods in code.

One of the key benefits of extending built-in controls in Delphi is the ability to encapsulate complex functionality within a single, reusable component. By creating custom controls that encapsulate specialized behavior, developers can simplify their code and reduce duplication, leading to more maintainable and scalable applications. Additionally, custom controls can be easily shared across projects and reused by other developers, further enhancing productivity and code reuse.

In addition to enhancing the visual appearance and behavior of standard controls, extending built-in controls in Delphi can also involve adding new functionality that is not available in the standard controls. For example, developers may need to create a custom data grid control that supports advanced sorting and filtering options, or a custom chart control that displays data in a specific format or layout.

To deploy custom controls in Delphi applications, developers typically package them into runtime packages (.bpl files) that can be dynamically linked to Delphi projects at design time or runtime. This allows developers to reuse and share custom controls across multiple projects without having to recompile or redistribute the entire application. Additionally, developers can distribute custom controls as standalone units (.pas files) or install them into the Delphi IDE using the Component Palette, making them readily available for use in new projects.

Overall, extending built-in controls for specialized functionality is a powerful technique in Delphi development that allows developers to create highly customizable and feature-rich applications. By leveraging the object-oriented nature of the language and the flexibility of the Delphi IDE, developers can build custom controls that meet the specific requirements of their applications while maintaining a high level of code reusability and maintainability. Whether it's enhancing the visual appearance of standard controls or adding new functionality, extending built-in controls in Delphi empowers developers to create rich and engaging user experiences.

Chapter 7: Implementing Design Patterns in Delphi Pascal

Design patterns are fundamental concepts in software engineering that provide reusable solutions to common problems encountered during the design and development of software applications. They encapsulate best practices and proven techniques for structuring and organizing code to achieve specific design goals, such as flexibility, scalability, and maintainability. Understanding design patterns is essential for developers looking to build robust and efficient software systems.

There are various categories of design patterns, each addressing different aspects of software design and architecture. One such category is creational patterns, which focus on object creation mechanisms, providing flexibility in object instantiation while promoting code reuse and maintainability. Examples of creational patterns include the Singleton pattern, which ensures that a class has only one instance and provides a global point of access to that instance, and the Factory Method pattern, which defines an interface for creating objects but allows subclasses to alter the type of objects that will be created.

Another category of design patterns is structural patterns, which deal with the composition of classes or objects to form larger structures while keeping the system flexible and efficient. Structural patterns include the Adapter pattern, which allows incompatible interfaces to work together by wrapping an interface around an existing class, and the Composite pattern, which composes objects into tree structures to represent part-whole hierarchies.

The third category of design patterns is behavioral patterns, which focus on communication between objects, defining how they interact and distribute responsibilities. Behavioral patterns include the Observer pattern, where an object, known as the subject, maintains a list of its dependents, called observers, and notifies them of any state changes, and the Strategy pattern, which defines a family of algorithms, encapsulates each one, and makes them interchangeable.

Design patterns can be applied at different levels of abstraction, ranging from low-level implementation details to high-level architectural decisions. They provide a common language and vocabulary for discussing and communicating design concepts among developers, facilitating collaboration and understanding within development teams. Moreover, design patterns promote code readability and maintainability by providing a standardized way of organizing and structuring code.

One of the key benefits of using design patterns is that they encapsulate proven solutions to recurring design problems, saving developers time and effort by eliminating the need to reinvent the wheel. By following established patterns, developers can leverage the collective wisdom of the software development community and build upon existing knowledge and experience.

Furthermore, design patterns promote code reusability and modularity, making it easier to maintain and extend software systems over time. By adhering to well-established patterns, developers can create code that is more robust, flexible, and adaptable to changing requirements, reducing the risk of introducing bugs or introducing unintended side effects.

However, it's essential to note that design patterns are not silver bullets and should be applied judiciously based on the specific needs and requirements of each project. Overusing patterns or applying them inappropriately can lead to overly complex and convoluted code, making it harder to understand and maintain. Therefore, it's crucial for developers to have a deep understanding of the underlying principles and trade-offs of each pattern and to apply them thoughtfully and selectively.

In summary, design patterns are essential tools in the software developer's toolbox, providing reusable solutions to common design problems and promoting best practices in software design and architecture. By understanding and applying design patterns effectively, developers can create software systems that are more robust, flexible, and maintainable, ultimately leading to higher-quality software products and more satisfied users.

Implementing common design patterns in Delphi applications is crucial for creating well-structured, maintainable, and scalable software solutions. Design patterns provide reusable solutions to recurring design problems, offering a standardized approach to software design and architecture. In Delphi, developers can leverage various design patterns to improve code organization, enhance code readability, and facilitate code maintenance.

One of the most commonly used design patterns in Delphi applications is the Singleton pattern. The Singleton pattern ensures that a class has only one instance and provides a global point of access to that instance. To implement the Singleton pattern in Delphi, developers can create a class with a private constructor and a static method that returns the single instance of the class. Additionally, developers can use a class variable to hold the single instance and initialize it lazily or eagerly based on the application's requirements.

Another widely used design pattern in Delphi is the Factory Method pattern. The Factory Method pattern defines an interface for creating objects but allows subclasses to alter the type of objects that will be created. In Delphi, developers can implement the Factory Method pattern by creating an abstract base class or interface that declares the factory method. Subclasses can then override the factory method to create instances of different concrete classes that implement the interface.

The Observer pattern is also commonly employed in Delphi applications to establish a one-to-many dependency between objects. The Observer pattern defines a subject that maintains a list of its dependents, called observers, and notifies them of any state changes. To implement the Observer pattern in Delphi, developers can create a subject class that maintains a list of observer objects and provides methods for adding, removing, and notifying observers of state changes. Observer objects can then register themselves with the subject and implement an update method to respond to notifications.

The Strategy pattern is another useful design pattern for implementing interchangeable algorithms in Delphi applications. The Strategy pattern defines a family of algorithms, encapsulates each one, and makes them interchangeable. In Delphi, developers can implement the Strategy pattern by creating a strategy interface or base class that declares the algorithm's contract. Concrete strategy classes can then implement the interface or extend the base class to provide different implementations of the algorithm.

The Decorator pattern is also applicable in Delphi applications for dynamically adding responsibilities to objects. The Decorator pattern attaches additional responsibilities to an object dynamically, providing a flexible alternative to subclassing for extending functionality. In Delphi, developers can implement the Decorator pattern by creating a base component interface or class and defining concrete components that implement the interface or extend the base class. Decorator classes can then wrap concrete components and add additional functionality without modifying their interface.

Moreover, the Command pattern is beneficial for encapsulating a request as an object, allowing developers to parameterize clients with queues, requests, and operations. The Command pattern decouples the sender of a request from the object that executes it, enabling developers to parameterize objects with operations and delay their execution or queue them for later execution. In Delphi, developers can implement the Command pattern by creating command interfaces or abstract base classes that declare execute methods. Concrete command classes can then implement the interfaces or extend the base classes to encapsulate specific requests and their corresponding operations.

Furthermore, the Iterator pattern is useful for accessing elements of a collection sequentially without exposing its underlying representation. The Iterator pattern decouples the collection's interface from its implementation, allowing developers to iterate over collections without knowing their internal structure. In Delphi, developers can implement the Iterator pattern by creating iterator interfaces or abstract base classes that declare methods for traversing collections. Concrete iterator classes can then implement the interfaces or extend the base classes to provide specific implementations for iterating over different types of collections.

Additionally, the Proxy pattern is beneficial for controlling access to an object by providing a surrogate or placeholder for it. The Proxy pattern allows developers to add additional functionality to an object without changing its interface, enabling lazy initialization, access control, logging, and monitoring. In Delphi, developers can implement the Proxy pattern by creating proxy classes that mimic the interface of the real object and delegate requests to it. Proxy classes can then add additional functionality before or after delegating requests to the real object.

In summary, implementing common design patterns in Delphi applications is essential for building robust, maintainable, and scalable software solutions. Design patterns provide reusable solutions to recurring design problems, offering a standardized approach to software design and architecture. By leveraging design patterns such as the Singleton, Factory Method, Observer, Strategy, Decorator, Command, Iterator, and Proxy patterns, developers can improve code organization, enhance code readability, and facilitate code maintenance in Delphi applications.

Chapter 8: Integrating Third-Party Libraries and Frameworks

Finding and evaluating third-party libraries is a crucial aspect of software development, enabling developers to leverage existing solutions and accelerate the development process. With the vast array of libraries available for different programming languages and frameworks, developers must navigate through various resources and criteria to identify the most suitable options for their projects.

One of the primary sources for finding third-party libraries is online repositories and package managers specific to the programming language or framework being used. For example, in the case of JavaScript development, npm (Node Package Manager) is a popular repository for JavaScript packages, while Python developers often rely on PyPI (Python Package Index). Similarly, for .NET development, NuGet serves as a central repository for .NET packages. Command-line tools such as npm, pip, and dotnet CLI provide convenient ways to search for and install packages directly from these repositories using commands like npm search, pip search, and dotnet add package.

In addition to package repositories, developers can also find third-party libraries on version control platforms such as GitHub, GitLab, and Bitbucket. These platforms host millions of open-source projects, including libraries and frameworks, allowing developers to browse through repositories, explore documentation, and evaluate community engagement. The git clone command can be used to clone repositories locally for further evaluation and integration into projects.

When evaluating third-party libraries, developers need to consider various factors to ensure compatibility, reliability, and maintainability. One crucial aspect is the library's documentation, which should provide clear instructions on installation, usage, and configuration. Comprehensive documentation with examples, API references, and troubleshooting guides can significantly streamline the integration process and help developers understand how to leverage the library's features effectively.

Another essential factor to consider is the library's license, as it dictates how the library can be used, modified, and distributed. Open-source licenses such as MIT, BSD, and Apache are generally permissive and allow for both commercial and non-commercial use with few restrictions. On the other hand, some licenses impose more stringent requirements or may not be compatible with certain project requirements. Developers can typically find information about a library's license in its documentation or repository's license file.

Community support and activity are also important considerations when evaluating third-party libraries. Active communities often indicate a healthy and well-maintained project, with frequent updates, bug fixes, and contributions from developers worldwide. Platforms like GitHub provide insights into a project's activity, including the number of stars, forks, and recent commits. Additionally, forums, mailing lists, and chat channels can be valuable resources for seeking help, reporting issues, and engaging with other users and contributors.

Furthermore, developers should assess the library's compatibility with their existing codebase and dependencies. Compatibility issues can arise due to differences in programming languages, runtime environments, or dependencies' versions. Library metadata and documentation typically specify compatibility requirements, including supported platforms, minimum required versions, and potential conflicts with other libraries.

Performance and efficiency are critical considerations, particularly for performance-sensitive applications or resource-constrained environments. Developers should evaluate a library's performance characteristics, including memory usage, CPU utilization, and execution speed, to ensure it meets their project's performance requirements. Benchmarking tools and performance profiling techniques can help assess a library's performance impact on different aspects of an application.

Security is another crucial aspect of evaluating third-party libraries, as vulnerabilities in dependencies can pose significant risks to applications. Developers should check for known security vulnerabilities in libraries using vulnerability databases such as the National Vulnerability Database (NVD) or vulnerability scanners integrated into package managers. Additionally, developers should regularly update dependencies to apply security patches and mitigate potential risks.

Finally, developers should consider the long-term viability and maintenance of third-party libraries before integrating them into their projects. Libraries with active maintainers, frequent updates, and a roadmap for future development are more likely to remain relevant and supported over time. Conversely, libraries that are abandoned or have no recent activity may pose risks in terms of compatibility, security, and long-term maintenance.

In summary, finding and evaluating third-party libraries is a crucial aspect of software development, enabling developers to leverage existing solutions and accelerate the development process. By considering factors such as documentation quality, license compatibility, community support, compatibility, performance, security, and long-term maintenance, developers can make informed decisions when selecting libraries for their projects. Command-line tools, online repositories, version control platforms, documentation, community forums, and automated testing and profiling tools are valuable resources for finding, evaluating, and integrating third-party libraries into software projects.

Integrating external libraries into Delphi projects is a fundamental aspect of software development, enabling developers to extend the functionality of their applications and leverage existing solutions to accelerate development. Delphi, a powerful programming language and integrated development environment (IDE) developed by Embarcadero Technologies, provides various mechanisms for incorporating external libraries, including dynamic-link libraries (DLLs), static libraries (LIBs), and packages (DCUs). These libraries can encompass a wide range of functionalities, from user interface components and data access layers to cryptographic algorithms and machine learning models.

One common approach to integrating external libraries into Delphi projects is by utilizing dynamic-link libraries (DLLs). DLLs are shared libraries containing executable code and data that can be dynamically loaded and linked into an application at runtime. Delphi provides built-in support for calling functions from DLLs using the external directive in function declarations. Developers can use the LoadLibrary function from the Windows API to load a DLL into memory and obtain a handle to the library, followed by the GetProcAddress function to retrieve the address of a specific function within the DLL. Once the function address is obtained, it can be invoked like any other Delphi function, passing parameters and receiving return values as needed.

Another approach for integrating external libraries into Delphi projects is by linking against static libraries (LIBs). Static libraries are archives of object files that contain precompiled code and can be linked directly into an application during the compilation process. Delphi supports linking against static libraries using the {$L} compiler directive, which instructs the compiler to include the specified LIB file in the compilation process. Once linked, the functions and symbols defined in the static library can be used directly within the Delphi project, similar to built-in functions and procedures.

In addition to DLLs and static libraries, Delphi also supports the concept of packages (DCUs) for modularizing and distributing reusable components and libraries. A Delphi package is a collection of compiled units (DCUs) that can be dynamically loaded and linked into an application at runtime. Packages provide a convenient way to encapsulate and distribute components, controls, and libraries, allowing developers to easily share and reuse code across multiple projects. Delphi IDE includes tools for creating, compiling, and installing packages, making it straightforward to integrate third-party components and libraries into Delphi projects. The Package Editor in Delphi IDE allows developers to specify package dependencies, export symbols, and define installation options, providing fine-grained control over the package's behavior and integration with other projects.

Furthermore, Delphi developers can integrate external libraries that are distributed as source code by including the source files directly in their projects. This approach allows developers to customize and extend the functionality of the library to meet their specific requirements while maintaining full control over the integration process. Delphi's powerful compiler and integrated development environment provide advanced code editing, refactoring, and debugging features that facilitate working with large codebases and external dependencies. Additionally, Delphi's support for object-oriented programming (OOP) principles such as inheritance, encapsulation, and polymorphism enables developers to create flexible and maintainable codebases that seamlessly integrate with external libraries and components.

When integrating external libraries into Delphi projects, developers should consider factors such as library compatibility, licensing, documentation, and support. It's essential to ensure that the library is compatible with the Delphi version being used and that any dependencies are met to avoid runtime errors and compatibility issues.

Additionally, developers should review the library's license to ensure compliance with their project's licensing requirements and to understand any restrictions on usage, distribution, and modification. Comprehensive documentation and support resources are also critical for successfully integrating external libraries, as they provide guidance on installation, configuration, usage, and troubleshooting.

In summary, integrating external libraries into Delphi projects is a vital aspect of software development, enabling developers to extend the functionality of their applications and leverage existing solutions to accelerate development. Delphi provides various mechanisms for integrating external libraries, including dynamic-link libraries (DLLs), static libraries (LIBs), packages (DCUs), and source code inclusion. By leveraging these mechanisms and considering factors such as library compatibility, licensing, documentation, and support, developers can effectively integrate external libraries into their Delphi projects and create robust and feature-rich applications.

Chapter 9: Designing for Accessibility and Internationalization

Ensuring accessibility in Delphi applications is a critical aspect of software development, as it enables users with disabilities to access and interact with the application effectively. Accessibility encompasses various aspects, including providing support for assistive technologies, adhering to accessibility standards and guidelines, and designing user interfaces that are perceivable, operable, and understandable by all users, regardless of their abilities. Delphi, a powerful programming language and integrated development environment (IDE) developed by Embarcadero Technologies, provides developers with tools and techniques to create accessible applications that comply with accessibility standards such as the Web Content Accessibility Guidelines (WCAG) and the Americans with Disabilities Act (ADA).

One essential aspect of ensuring accessibility in Delphi applications is providing support for assistive technologies such as screen readers, magnifiers, and alternative input devices. Screen readers, for example, are software programs that read aloud the content of the screen to users who are blind or visually impaired. Delphi applications can support screen readers by providing meaningful names and descriptions for user interface elements such as buttons, labels, and text boxes, using the AccessibleName and AccessibleDescription properties available in Delphi's visual components. Additionally, developers can use the AccessibleRole property to specify the role of each user interface element, such as button, link, or text box, to assist screen readers in interpreting and navigating the application's user interface.

Another aspect of ensuring accessibility in Delphi applications is adhering to accessibility standards and guidelines such as WCAG and ADA. These standards define criteria and best practices for making web content and applications accessible to users with disabilities, including requirements for perceivable content, operable user interfaces, understandable information, and robust implementation. Delphi developers can ensure compliance with accessibility standards by following guidelines such as providing text alternatives for non-text content, ensuring keyboard accessibility, avoiding color-based information, and designing user interfaces that are consistent and predictable in their behavior.

Furthermore, designing user interfaces that are perceivable, operable, and understandable by all users is essential for ensuring accessibility in Delphi applications. This includes considerations such as providing sufficient color contrast for text and background elements to enhance readability for users with low vision or color blindness, ensuring that user interface controls are keyboard accessible and operable without relying on mouse interactions, and providing clear and concise instructions and error messages that are understandable by users with cognitive disabilities or limited literacy skills. Delphi's visual components provide properties and events that enable developers to customize the appearance and behavior of user interface elements to meet accessibility requirements, such as setting the TabStop property to enable keyboard navigation and specifying Hint messages to provide additional context or instructions for user interface controls.

Moreover, testing and evaluating the accessibility of Delphi applications is an essential step in ensuring that they meet the needs of all users. Developers can use accessibility testing tools and assistive technologies to assess the accessibility of their applications, identify potential barriers or usability issues, and make necessary improvements to enhance accessibility. Delphi IDE provides features such as the Object Inspector and the Structure View, which allow developers to inspect and navigate the hierarchy of visual components in their applications and verify that accessibility properties are properly configured. Additionally, developers can use third-party accessibility testing tools and screen readers to evaluate the accessibility of their applications from the perspective of users with disabilities.

In summary, ensuring accessibility in Delphi applications is essential for providing inclusive and equitable access to information and services for users with disabilities. Delphi provides developers with tools and techniques to create accessible applications that comply with accessibility standards and guidelines, support assistive technologies, and provide perceivable, operable, and understandable user interfaces. By following best practices for accessibility and testing the accessibility of their applications, Delphi developers can create software that meets the needs of all users and promotes inclusivity and diversity in the digital world.

Internationalizing Delphi applications for global markets is a crucial step in ensuring that software products can effectively reach and cater to users from diverse linguistic and cultural backgrounds. Internationalization, often abbreviated as "i18n," involves designing and developing applications in a way that enables easy adaptation to different languages, regions, and cultural conventions without requiring extensive code changes. Delphi, a robust programming language and integrated development environment (IDE) developed by Embarcadero Technologies, provides developers with tools and techniques to internationalize their applications effectively and efficiently.

One essential aspect of internationalizing Delphi applications is designing user interfaces (UI) that support multilingual content and accommodate variations in text length and format. Delphi's visual components, such as labels, buttons, and menus, support Unicode characters, enabling developers to display text in various languages and character sets without encoding issues. Additionally, developers can use resource strings or external localization files to store translatable text strings separately from the application code, making it easier to translate and localize the application for different languages and regions.

Another aspect of internationalizing Delphi applications is supporting locale-specific conventions for date and time formatting, numeric representation, and currency symbols. Delphi provides functions and classes to format date and time values according to different cultural norms and user preferences, such as the FormatDateTime function and the TFormatSettings record, which allow developers to specify locale-specific formatting options. Similarly, Delphi's FormatFloat function enables developers to format numeric values according to locale-specific conventions, including decimal and thousand separators and currency symbols.

Furthermore, internationalizing Delphi applications involves adapting user interface elements and content to cultural preferences and sensitivities. This includes considerations such as using culturally appropriate imagery, icons, and symbols, avoiding text or graphics that may be offensive or inappropriate in certain cultures, and ensuring that user interface layouts and interactions align with cultural expectations and norms. Delphi's visual components and design tools provide flexibility for developers to customize the appearance and behavior of user interface elements to suit different cultural contexts and user preferences.

Moreover, internationalizing Delphi applications requires testing and validation to ensure that the software functions correctly and is culturally appropriate in different linguistic and cultural environments. Developers can use localization testing tools and techniques to verify that translated text strings fit within UI elements and do not cause layout or formatting issues. Additionally, testing with users from different language and cultural backgrounds can provide valuable feedback on the usability and cultural appropriateness of the application.

In summary, internationalizing Delphi applications is essential for reaching global markets and providing users with a localized and culturally appropriate experience. Delphi provides developers with tools and techniques to internationalize their applications effectively, including support for multilingual content, locale-specific formatting, and culturally sensitive design. By following best practices for internationalization and testing the application in different linguistic and cultural environments, Delphi developers can create software products that are accessible and relevant to users worldwide.

Chapter 10: Optimizing Performance and Scalability in Delphi Applications

Performance optimization techniques are crucial for ensuring that software applications deliver optimal speed, responsiveness, and efficiency. In the context of software development, optimizing performance involves identifying and eliminating bottlenecks, reducing resource consumption, and improving overall system responsiveness. Delphi, a powerful programming language and integrated development environment (IDE) developed by Embarcadero Technologies, provides developers with a range of tools and techniques to optimize the performance of their applications effectively.

One fundamental aspect of performance optimization in Delphi applications is identifying and addressing computational bottlenecks. Profiling tools such as AQtime and Sampling Profiler can help developers identify areas of code that consume excessive CPU cycles or memory, allowing them to focus their optimization efforts on the most critical areas. Once bottlenecks are identified, developers can use techniques such as algorithm optimization, data structure optimization, and code refactoring to improve the efficiency of the affected code paths.

Algorithm optimization involves analyzing and improving the efficiency of algorithms used in the application. This may involve replacing inefficient algorithms with more efficient ones, reducing the time complexity of algorithms by optimizing loops and conditional statements, and minimizing redundant or unnecessary computations. For example, developers can use hashing or memoization techniques to optimize repetitive calculations and improve overall algorithm performance.

Data structure optimization focuses on selecting and designing data structures that are optimized for specific use cases and operations. Delphi provides a variety of built-in data structures, such as arrays, lists, sets, maps, and queues, each with its own strengths and weaknesses. By choosing the appropriate data structure for each scenario and optimizing data access patterns, developers can reduce memory usage, improve cache locality, and optimize data retrieval and manipulation operations.

Code refactoring involves restructuring and rewriting code to improve its readability, maintainability, and performance. This may include simplifying complex code, eliminating redundant or duplicated code, and optimizing critical code paths for performance. Delphi's refactoring tools, such as the built-in Refactoring menu and third-party refactoring plugins, provide developers with automated refactorings for common optimization tasks, such as extracting methods, inlining variables, and optimizing imports.

Another important aspect of performance optimization in Delphi applications is minimizing memory usage and managing resource consumption efficiently. Delphi's memory management system, based on reference counting and garbage collection, automatically deallocates memory when it is no longer in use, reducing the risk of memory leaks and resource exhaustion. However, developers must still be mindful of memory allocation patterns, object lifetimes, and resource usage to avoid excessive memory consumption and performance degradation.

Furthermore, optimizing I/O operations, such as file I/O, database access, and network communication, is essential for improving the performance of Delphi applications. Techniques such as asynchronous I/O, batch processing, connection pooling, and caching can help reduce latency, improve throughput, and minimize the impact of I/O bottlenecks on application performance. Delphi provides libraries and components for working with various data sources and communication protocols, allowing developers to optimize I/O operations for specific use cases and performance requirements.

Moreover, optimizing the user interface (UI) and improving the responsiveness of Delphi applications can enhance the overall user experience and perception of performance. Techniques such as lazy loading, virtualization, background processing, and UI thread management can help reduce UI latency, prevent blocking operations, and ensure smooth and responsive interaction with the application. Delphi's multi-threading support and asynchronous programming features enable developers to parallelize and distribute computational tasks across multiple threads, improving overall system responsiveness and performance.

In summary, performance optimization techniques are essential for ensuring that Delphi applications deliver optimal speed, efficiency, and responsiveness. By identifying and addressing computational bottlenecks, optimizing algorithms and data structures, minimizing memory usage, optimizing I/O operations, and improving UI responsiveness, developers can create high-performance Delphi applications that meet the performance requirements and expectations of users.

Scaling Delphi applications for high-demand environments is crucial for ensuring that they can handle increased workloads, user concurrency, and data processing requirements without sacrificing performance or reliability. In today's digital landscape, where applications must support thousands or even millions of users concurrently, scalability is a critical consideration for developers building Delphi applications. Scaling an application involves optimizing its architecture, infrastructure, and codebase to accommodate growing demand while maintaining acceptable levels of performance, availability, and responsiveness.

One of the key considerations when scaling Delphi applications is designing a scalable architecture that can accommodate increased traffic and workload. This often involves adopting a distributed architecture, where different components of the application are deployed across multiple servers or cloud instances to distribute the load and prevent single points of failure. Delphi developers can leverage technologies such as microservices, containers, and serverless computing to break down monolithic applications into smaller, more manageable components that can be scaled independently based on demand.

Containerization, using tools like Docker, allows developers to package applications and their dependencies into lightweight, portable containers that can be deployed consistently across different environments. By containerizing Delphi applications, developers can streamline the deployment process, improve scalability, and enhance resource utilization. Additionally, container orchestration platforms such as Kubernetes provide automated scaling capabilities, allowing Delphi applications to dynamically adjust their resource allocation based on demand.

Another important aspect of scaling Delphi applications is optimizing database performance and scalability. As application traffic increases, database bottlenecks can emerge, leading to slow query performance, increased latency, and reduced throughput. Delphi developers can address these challenges by optimizing database schema design, indexing, query optimization, and caching strategies to improve database performance and scalability. Additionally, leveraging distributed databases, caching layers, and replication techniques can help distribute the database workload and improve overall scalability.

Furthermore, caching frequently accessed data and computations can significantly improve the performance and scalability of Delphi applications. By caching data at various layers of the application stack, such as in-memory caches, distributed caches, or content delivery networks (CDNs), developers can reduce the need for repeated computations and database queries, resulting in faster response times and improved scalability. Delphi provides libraries and components for implementing caching mechanisms, such as the TCache class and third-party caching libraries, enabling developers to optimize application performance and scalability.

Additionally, optimizing network communication and resource utilization is essential for scaling Delphi applications effectively. This involves minimizing latency, reducing network overhead, and optimizing data transfer protocols to ensure efficient communication between application components. Delphi developers can leverage techniques such as connection pooling, asynchronous communication, and message queueing to improve network performance and scalability. Using protocols like HTTP/2 and WebSockets can also help reduce latency and improve real-time communication capabilities in Delphi applications.

Moreover, automating deployment and management processes is essential for scaling Delphi applications efficiently. Continuous integration and continuous deployment (CI/CD) pipelines enable developers to automate the build, test, and deployment process, ensuring that changes are deployed quickly and reliably. Delphi developers can use CI/CD tools such as Jenkins, TeamCity, or GitLab CI/CD to automate the deployment of application updates and scale deployments seamlessly across multiple environments.

Furthermore, monitoring and performance tuning are ongoing processes that are essential for maintaining the scalability and reliability of Delphi applications over time. By monitoring key performance metrics such as CPU usage, memory utilization, response times, and error rates, developers can identify performance bottlenecks and proactively address them before they impact the user experience. Delphi developers can use monitoring tools such as Prometheus, Grafana, and New Relic to monitor application performance and diagnose scalability issues in real-time.

In summary, scaling Delphi applications for high-demand environments requires careful planning, optimization, and automation across all layers of the application stack. By designing a scalable architecture, optimizing database performance, caching frequently accessed data, optimizing network communication, automating deployment processes, and monitoring application performance, Delphi developers can build applications that can handle increased traffic, user concurrency, and data processing requirements while maintaining optimal performance and reliability.

Conclusion

In the comprehensive book bundle "Delphi Pascal Programming: Efficient Code Editing, Visual Designing, and Integrated Debugging," readers are equipped with a holistic understanding of Delphi Pascal programming, from mastering the essentials to fine-tuning skills for expert-level proficiency. Across four books, this bundle covers a spectrum of topics essential for developers seeking to excel in Delphi Pascal programming.

Book 1, "Delphi Pascal Programming Essentials: Mastering Efficient Code Editing," lays the foundation by providing readers with essential techniques and best practices for writing clean, maintainable code. From leveraging powerful code editing features to optimizing productivity with shortcuts and customizations, readers learn how to streamline their coding workflow and produce high-quality software efficiently.

In Book 2, "From Basics to Brilliance: Visual Designing in Delphi Pascal Programming," readers embark on a journey to master visual design principles and techniques within the Delphi IDE. Through practical examples and hands-on exercises, developers learn how to create visually stunning user interfaces that enhance user experience and engagement. From layout and alignment strategies to integrating graphics and animations, this book empowers readers to design compelling UIs that captivate users.

Book 3, "Advanced Techniques in Delphi Pascal: Integrated Debugging Strategies," delves into the intricacies of debugging, offering readers advanced strategies for identifying, diagnosing, and resolving software defects. With a focus on integrated debugging tools and techniques within the Delphi IDE, developers learn how to effectively troubleshoot and debug complex applications, ensuring optimal performance and reliability.

Finally, Book 4, "Delphi Pascal Programming Pro: Fine-Tuning Code Editing and Visual Designing for Experts," caters to seasoned professionals seeking to elevate their Delphi programming skills to the next level. Through advanced topics and expert-level insights, readers gain a deeper understanding of code editing, visual designing, and debugging, enabling them to tackle even the most challenging projects with confidence and precision.

Collectively, this book bundle equips readers with the knowledge, skills, and techniques needed to excel in Delphi Pascal programming. Whether you are a novice developer looking to master the essentials or an experienced professional seeking to refine your expertise, "Delphi Pascal Programming" provides a comprehensive resource to help you achieve your goals and unlock your full potential in the world of software development.